LEADING
SALES
DEVELOPMENT

THE ART
AND SCIENCE OF
BUILDING EXCEPTIONAL TEAMS

ALEA HOMISON AND JEREMEY DONOVAN

CONTENTS

INTRODUCTION

This is a book about the roles of art and science in building and culti-
vating high-performing sales development teams - teams that consistently deliver results, that successfully groom future AE talent, that become
families of diverse talent, and that despite their success, are never satisfied.

If art seems like an unusual term to use in a business book, let us
explain why it is important here. We like the term "art" because art is the
creative way in which we apply what we've learned through our many years
of combined experiences in strategy and sales at marquee enterprises and
hyper-growth startups, including Credit Suisse, Abercrombie & Fitch,
Gartner, GLG, AlphaSense, and SalesLoft. These learned experiences gave
us the insight and ability to enjoy many business successes from which
we are able to share with you here in what we call best practice. However,
there were also some knowledge-building failures that were also important
in adding to our knowledge that we will also share and refer to as "les-
sons-learned." Another aspect that contributed greatly to this art of setting
up high-performing sales teams comes from what we continue to learn
through speaking with peers who lead sales development diverse companies. In addition, we would be remiss if we didn't share the great ideas we
have been able to cull from other authors by voraciously reading as many
sales books as possible.

The science comes from our academic foundations in business and
engineering as much as it does from our skepticism. When evaluating ideas

to test, whether from our own minds, those of our peers, or from books, it is common practice for us to question even the most basic assumptions -- because the stakes high. When we get things wrong, we put our companies at risk. But more than that, we put our sales development representatives (SDRs) at risk. For many of the people on our teams, this is their first or second job and we bear a deep responsibility to help them develop into tomorrow's exceptional account executives and sales leaders. We take this responsibility of professional development seriously.

So you see, the marriage of art and science in this book happens when we validate an idea against academic research and commercial studies. Throughout the book, we will cite the studies that support or refute ideas for leading sales development and even delve into "SDR math," particularly basic algebra and statistics. However, do not think of this book as a textbook. We wrote it in an accessible and casual tone. Just as we question everything in our lives, we made every effort to explain complex concepts in everyday conversational language assuming that you, our reader, shares in our curiosity.

Yet, this is also a book written by active practitioners for active practitioners. Compared with books written by sales consultants (many of which are excellent), we have no agenda other than providing guidance to elevate the B2B sales profession. We do not "sell-from-the-page" by directly or implicitly promoting ourselves or our companies. Nor do we claim to invent new methodologies by disingenuously renaming foundational frameworks, as do so many others.

As practitioners, we are also practical. By this we mean two things: First, we have no interest in being provocative for its own sake. For instance, pundits get up on their high horses to shout, "Email is dead, long live Social Selling!", or "Sell value, never features," or other nonsense. Taking a provocative position usually means embracing a false dichotomy - implying something is a strict "OR" when in reality it is an "AND" or simply depends on context. The truth is success requires email and phone and social and other channels. The truth is prospects care more about value than features at some points in the buying process and more about features than value in other parts. Second, we apply systems-level thinking. To be actionable, insights must be plugged into imperfect organizations that have constraints on people, process, and technology.

In order to be most effective, we've divided the book into three parts with each part aligned with a strategic and operational levers sales development leaders can control.

Part I focuses on the art and science of selecting talent. Here you will learn which traits actually predict success and which traits sound important but really do not matter. You'll learn how to properly screen and test for those traits and how to interview the right way (Spoiler Alert: The way most companies teach managers to interview ignores decades of academic research that proves conventional methods yield no better results than throwing darts at resumes, blindfolded!).

Part II focuses on setting new hires up for success. Even successful SDRs are only in their jobs for about 18-24 months before being promoted to account executives. As such, sales development leaders must build well-oiled systems to onboard, train, and motivate their teams.

Part III delves into the nitty, gritty of accelerating performance. We go deep on how to design multi-touch, multi-channel cadences and on how to drive and measure performance.

Although this book is written primarily for managers and directors of sales development, we also believe aspiring sales development leaders, sales development reps interested in the broader context of their discipline, and chief revenue officers will also find it valuable. And, if you are an account executive or revenue operational professional who geeks out on B2B sales like we do, then we know you'll like it too.

Let's get started!

PART I

SELECTING TALENT

CHAPTER 1

Identifying the "Core Four" Talent Traits

Many factors can lead you to succeed as a sales development leader, but none is more important than the ability to recognize and draft talented individuals.onto your team Make no mistake, there is more to this than just hiring warm bodies, never forget that you are selecting colleagues who are worth your investment of time, money, effort, and care. Keep in mind, too, that your team must generate quality pipeline at an acceptable cost of sales inclusive of overhead, such as management (that's you), tools, etc., and that you have 18 months, give or take, to develop people able to succeed as account executives once they are promoted.

Let's start by reflecting for a moment on your firm's current hiring process. We are guessing it is semi-disciplined and looks something like this: Applicants reply to job postings through a variety of channels. Someone on your human resources team screens these applicants, though you are not exactly sure what questions they ask. Candidates who make it through the HR screening have an initial call with the hiring manager who is supposed to ask a prescribed set of questions. But what usually happens is this manager just got out of a meeting and barely had time to pull up the candidate's resume, let alone find the questions to ask. As a result, the hiring manager follows their instincts when conducting this initial call to which this manager gives the thumbs up to proceed to the next hiring phase. Before returning for a day of interviews, the candidate is given a personality test that either isn't reviewed or has no bearing on hiring. Finally, the candidate comes in for a few final back-to-back interviews meant to have structure, perhaps to explore competencies, but don't and the interviewers again go on gut, give their thumbs up, HR checks the candidate supplied two references and, voila, the person is on your team.

Sure, we're being a bit cynical, but we've been on both sides that type of hiring process enough times that it's a sure bet we got much of it correct. And we're here to tell you that that approach doesn't bode well for your ultimate success and that there is a better way. Like almost all effective processes, this new approach is not rocket science, but it does require disciplined adherence to every step, but it will pay off. The following Four Core Traits are designed to help you evaluate candidates in a way that will allow you to choose the right individuals critical to your team's future success. Okay we lied just a tiny little bit, we said no rocket science, but. we promise to make it painless.

Core Trait #1: General Mental Ability (GMA)

Years ago, in 1998 in fact, academics Frank Schmidt and John Hunter cracked the code on hiring by analyzing 85 years of data on 19 best (and worst) practices for personnel selection[1]. While this research is ripe for the taking, few professionals are aware of it. (One notable exception is Google, which rigorously applies the finding).

Schmidt and Hunter start by putting general mental ability (GMA) – aka cognitive ability, 'clock-speed,' or intelligence quotient (IQ) – on a pedestal because it is highly correlated ($r = 0.51$) with job performance, can be used for all jobs, is low cost, and demands little time on the part of the applicant to take and on the hiring organization to analyze.

While the researchers explored many types of jobs, we contend that GMA is especially critical to success in sales. Sales people must be able to build trust by adapting to prospects' questions on-the-fly, especially during nerve-rattling cold calls lasting anywhere from 30 seconds to 3 minutes. That means knowing your products and services, your customers, your competitors, and your sales process with the depth and nuance required to engage prospects in seamless and authentic conversation. Associates who need scripts to be successful do not survive in sales. Since only smart people need apply, GMA is the first of four core traits we look for in hiring.

In case statistics class is a little fuzzy in your memory, remember that correlation is the mutual relationship between two things, in this case GMA and job performance. Correlation does not imply causation. To prove causation, one must conduct a controlled study holding everything constant in two populations except for the one factor. Proving a causal relationship between GMA and job performance will remain elusive, since we would have to clone not only people but also their experiences prior to and during the study. Hence, we will just have to be content with correlation.

One more important statistics factoid. The square of the correlation coefficient ($R2$ or R-squared) represents the amount of variation in one variable explained by variation in the other variable. Hence, a correlation $r = 0.51$ means that 26% of variation in job performance is explained by variation in GMA. That number may seem low, but by social science standards it is very, very strong.

Take a moment to think through the implications. Businesses spend billions upon billions of dollars, countless hours, and endless effort evaluating candidates. Precious few administer GMA tests. Yet, those tests are by far the best predictor of job performance from a cost-benefit point of view.

The researchers don't explicitly compute this, but if we were able to conduct all 19 tests on a group of exceptionally patient candidates, we would be able to predict up to 50% of the variation in job performance. But, before you dismiss 50-50 as bad, the alternative is throwing darts at a resumes on a board, which is an apt metaphor for the way most organizations hire.

Assuming we've made a compelling case for GMA, you should be asking one of two questions: The first is "What are the other two core traits we look for when hiring?" The second is "How exactly do you go about assessing GMA?" Please note that we tackle these questions in numerical order, so if you are champing at the bit for the 'how-to', be patient. The reason is because many steps in our recommended selection process test multiple traits at once.

Core Trait #2: Curiosity

Curiosity is the second core trait we look for when selecting talent which means that GMA, the ability to process information, is useless unless a person routinely feeds their active curious mind.

Consciously or subconsciously, the best hires know their success depends on their knowledge of your products and of what is top-of-mind for your customers. An incurious person will sit through training and role play and complete their assignments – they'll "check the box". In contrast, curious people go deeper on all of these. They will be the ones in the front row of the class asking challenging questions. They will be the ones that run the role play tape in their minds over and over, not because they think they messed up but because they want to understand the psychology of what worked and what did not work. They will be the ones that seek out the stars in your company (and beyond) as informal mentors. And, they will be the ones that consume industry news and information of their own volition in order to establish trust and add value in their interactions with prospects.

Though Schmidt and Hunter did not consider curiosity, another academic, Patrick Mussel built on their work[2]. Mussel started by determining the amount of variation (R2) in job performance explained by GMA, obtaining similar results as his predecessors. Adding curiosity to the mix, Mussel calculated an incremental 7% increase in R2. Once again, in the realm of social science, that is a dramatic increase that serves to solidify curiosity as a core hiring trait.

Core Trait #3: Conscientiousness

As you probably suspected, we did not pull conscientiousness out of thin air. Schmidt and Hunter found that possessing this trait increases predicted variation in job performance by 10% over GMA alone.

Having collectively managed hundreds of people, we both noticed the best associates hold themselves accountable to tasks and goals., When selecting talent, we think of conscientiousness as a more evolved version of competitiveness; conscientious people compete against their own daily, weekly, monthly, and quarterly best performances. They are focused on how to be better today than they were yesterday.

Jack Fraser, an exemplar of this trait, achieved the production goals required to get promoted from SDR to AE in 11 months, the fastest in SalesLoft history. Since Jack's will was so strong, his manager's job was to feed him great accounts and to coach him on activity quality. As managers, we love self-motivated people, since it is never pleasant to hound people into achieving minimum activity standards. Moreover, we trust conscientious people like Jack by giving them more autonomy – something we know they appreciate.

Core Trait #4: Grit

Since we are seeking to convey timeless traits, we had a minor disagreement about whether to include grit, given its trendiness. It's very concept was introduced to the academic establishment back in 2007, in a paper entitled, "Grit: Perseverance and Passion for Long-Term Goals.[3]" It then took the business world by storm when Angela Duckworth, the article's lead author, published her business bestseller "Grit: The Power of Passion and Perseverance" in 2016.

We obviously believe passion and perseverance are critical traits, however, the ultimate question is whether they are subsumed by more well-established personality traits. Our cause for concern is the existence of ongoing debate surrounding another popular construct, Emotional

Intelligence (EQ). Specifically, psychology researchers continue to test whether EQ is just convenient repackaging of the long-established and well-accepted "Big 5" model:

- Conscientiousness (versus carelessness)

- Openness to experience (versus cautiousness)

- Extraversion (versus introversion)

- Agreeableness (versus argumentativeness)

- Neuroticism (versus emotional stability)

Fortunately, the original 2007 paper addresses this concern. Duckworth and her colleagues conducted six studies. We will briefly describe the one addressing why grit is the Big 5 model. So we do not drag you too far into the weeds, note that the other studies found grit to be relatively independent of IQ (aka GMA).

In the study exploring grit and the Big 5 model, the researchers set up a link to a popular website[4] where visitors could complete a grit self-assessment. The test includes questions like "New ideas and projects sometimes distract me from previous ones" and "I am a hard worker." Respondents select answers on a 5-level scale from "Not at all like me" to "Very much like me." (You can access the current 10 question Grit Scale for free at https://angeladuckworth.com/grit-scale/). In addition to the grit self-assessment, 706 participants also completed a Big 5 personality test and indicated the number of times they had switched careers. While they found grit strongly related to conscientiousness and, to a lesser extent, the other Core Four factors, they nonetheless found "grit had incremental predictive validity for number of lifetime career changes over and beyond age, conscientiousness, and other Big 5 traits.... Individuals who where a standard deviation higher in grit than average were 35% less likely to be frequent career switchers."

The reason we share this research should now be apparent--we strive to hire salespeople who will stay with our companies. The Center for

American Progress reviewed dozens of case studies and research papers and found the typical cost of turnover is about 20% of an employee's annual salary[5]. That amounts to $12,000 to $16,000 for an SDR making between $60,000 and $80,000. However, we feel the costs of sales professional turnover are likely much higher when you consider lost pipeline while selecting and ramping replacement hires.

With grit now a safe candidate for inclusion as a core selection trait, we can reflect further on its components, those of perseverance and passion, for long-term goals. On the former, we would argue that prospecting is the most soul-consuming job in sales. Day-in and day-out, SDRs must make 50 or more phone calls and send 50 or more emails to book just one meeting on average. It takes perseverance to keep on keeping on when you are ignored, get hung-up on, and ultimately rejected.

We all want to hire people who want to be in the sales profession rather than people still trying to figure out what it is they want to do. That said, we welcome career switchers from other disciplines. One of our best former associates, Nitisha Shrestha, previously worked in human resources as a recruiter. Months after joining our sales development team, she walked in one morning with a smile on her face and said, "This is the first time in my career that I love coming to work." We need people with this same mindset and way of thinking that comes largely from within.

We want candidates to at least think they are going to love sales; otherwise, they will be very hard to motivate. One must love sales for rare, ecstatic highs to make up for consistent lows. Even though SDRs typically get promoted to AE in 18 to 24 months, so many of them fail partway through and flee the sales profession into careers with more stability but far lower long-term earning potential. We want people that are not going down without a fight. People that will push through the inevitable tough times and prove to everyone, including themselves, that they have what it takes to be successful in sales.

In Summary...

A discussion thread on Modern Sales Pros, one of our favorite forums for best practice sharing, began with "The Best Salespeople in the world are..." After the dust settled, we boiled the list down as follows:

- GMA (IQ, clock-speed, cognitive ability, intelligence)
- Curiosity (coachability, learning, inquisitiveness)
- Conscientiousness (competitiveness, discipline, organization, consistency)
- Grit (tenacity, drive, relentlessness, work ethic, initiative, passion, achievement/goal orientation, perseverance, courage, patience, positivity, optimism)
- Other
  - Assertiveness, Confidence
  - Empathy, compassion, customer-centricity, service, responsiveness, self-awareness, emotional intelligence
  - Humility, modesty, likeability
  - Creativity

As you can see from the above list, there are at least 4 other traits we ignored. We decided not to have 8 Core Traits because it is (next to) impossible to accurately and consistently measure more than a few traits for every candidate; even four push the limit. In addition, as much as we like them, we do not have the science to prove that any of those additional traits are statistically correlated with job performance. Given the challenge and the lack of hard data, we stand by our "Core Four" traits.

Now that you know what traits explain variation on job performance, the next chapter will show you how to detect those traits in job candidates.

CHAPTER 2
Screening Resumes

We will admit that devoting an entire chapter on resume screening may seem excessive, however, when you consider that hiring managers probably spend more time in aggregate reviewing resumes than they do interviewing candidates and that few, if any, were ever trained to look at the essential traits, this chapter makes perfect business sense.

Furthermore, we believe it is imperative that managers carve out time to personally screen resumes rather than having HR 'pre-screen' because the top of the talent funnel is such a critical hiring lever. If your organization has the luxury of drowning in resumes, then ensure your recruiting team is fully aligned with your hiring principles, preferably ones directly informed by those you are about to learn in this chapter.

In our experience, every manager tends to come up with an idiosyncratic set of criteria based on what they believe matters. We will do our best to make the time you spend reading this chapter well worth your time as we present both sides of the science vs. gut intuition arguments. To keep ourselves honest, we weave our "Core Four" Traits (GMA, Curiosity, Conscientiousness, Grit) into the discussion to help us deconstruct the three parts of any resume: Education, Work Experience, and Activities in our quest to select the best SDR talent.

EDUCATION

Does it matter where SDRs went to college?

Imagine one could identify every person who had ever been an SDR, know the college they attended, and, most importantly, know whether that person had been successful in the role. Even though that specific task is an impossibility, we found a reasonable substitute.

Rather than finding every former SDR, we looked only at one company. We chose a company that has employed many SDRs, and that had been continuously successful, in order to eliminate as many factors out of SDRs' control as possible. Our obvious choice, Salesforce, had employed 1,799 SDRs at the time we pulled the data from LinkedIn. By using LinkedIn to find the people, it was also easy to collect their educational background data.

The hard part came in defining what it meant to be successful in the role, especially since we did not have access to hyper-sensitive personnel data. We solved this by defining success as having been promoted from SDR to AE at Salesforce. This seemed logical as advancement to quota-carrying sales professional is one of the main two goals of having a sales development team (the other goal is, of course, being to generate quality pipeline). We kept the success definition strict, ignoring SDRs who were promoted into other roles at Salesforce or who moved into AE roles at other companies.

Sacrificing a bit of data to gain relevancy for most readers, we isolated former Salesforce SDRs based in the United States, yielding 739 people. Of these, 76.3% were successful in earning a promotion to AE at the company.

For school quality, we turned to undergraduate rankings from Forbes. The results, grouped by range for convenience, are shown in Figure 2.1.

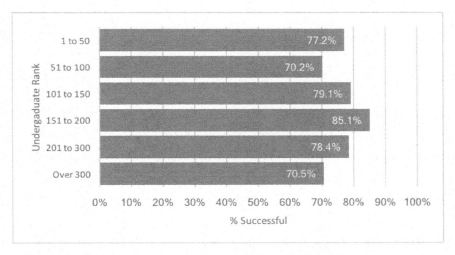

Figure 2.1 Success rate of Salesforce SDRs vs. Undergraduate Rank

If school rank truly mattered, it seemed logical that people who attended higher ranked institutions would have higher success rates. Figure 2.1 disproved that, at least for the decent sample we looked at. Attending a high-ranking school did not impact a person's future success as a salesperson.

We looked at this same type of data for Fortune 1000 CEOs and Inc. 5000 entrepreneurs and found the same result. Why? There are too many variables ranging from maturity exhibited between the ages of 14 and 17; parents' income; geographic preferences/constraints, etc. These factors blur the correlation between academic ranking and the four core traits that lead to success.

Does college major matter for SDRs?

Next, we grouped college majors into four buckets

- Business: Accounting, Economics, Finance, Marketing, etc.

- Humanities: Arts, Communication, English, History, Psychology, etc.

- Political Science

- STEM: Science, Technology, Engineering, and Mathematics

As you have probably gathered by now, anything perceived is not accurate enough for us because we know full too well that you are responsible for making important decisions that affect not only your company but your own career, and the careers of many others. Therefore, to even begin to formulate a hypothesis based on whether a person's college major matters we need to find a link between GMA and major. Fortunately, data attributed to Educational Testing Service[6] (ETS) yielded the following – IQ in parentheses: STEM (126), Political Science (120), Business (114), and Humanities (114).

Given the IQ versus academic degree data, we would expect individuals with STEM degrees to be the most successful as SDRs, followed by those with political science degrees, followed by a tie between those with Business or Humanities degrees. Figure 2.2 closely confirms our expectation, though STEM stands out, with the other three degree groups more or less tied.

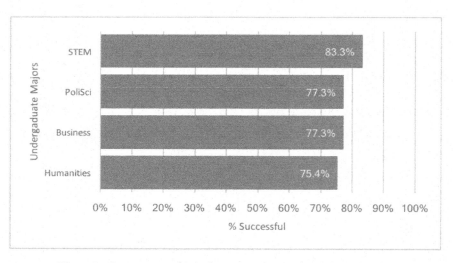

Figure 2.2 Success rate of Salesforce SDRs vs. Undergraduate Degree

In theory, this finding suggests we should rush to hire people with STEM degrees. While this is wise counsel, the practical reality is that B2B sales is not (currently) a highly desirable career path for engineers and

14

mathematicians; cream-of-the-crop graduates in those fields have much higher early-career earning potential in information technology and finance. Actual percentages by major at Salesforce confirms that SDRs with STEM degrees are rare: STEM (5%); Political Science (7%); Business (57%), and Humanities (31%). Hence, keep a keen eye open for STEM graduates looking to move into sales, but don't make this your hiring strategy unless you are willing to pay starting salaries 50% to 100% (or even higher) than SDRs usually command. In turn, this would most likely lead to an unpalatable and unprofitable cost of sales.

Does college grade point average (GPA) matter?

Unfortunately, very few people put their GPA on their LinkedIn profile and we did not bother reaching out to those 739 people to ask. To the reasonable extent that GPA links to at least three of the four core traits (GMA, Conscientiousness, and Grit), we'd expect GPA to predict SDR success.

The best we can do here is cite Lazlo Bock, Google's former Senior Vice President of People Operations, quote in the New York Times,[7] "After two or three years, your ability to perform at Google is completely unrelated to how you performed when you were in school, because the skills you required in college are very different. You're also fundamentally a different person. You learn and grow, you think about things differently."

It is logical then to turn this quote around and assume that GPA very likely does matter for early career professionals–usually the exact profile of those hired into SDR roles. For people with more than three years of work experience, it is a better bet to ignore education and focus instead on work experience, as we conveniently do next.

WORK EXPERIENCE

Does prior work experience matter?

One of the most striking things we found in looking at the Salesforce SDR success data was that 87% worked after college and before they were hired by Salesforce. That high of a percentage loudly signals strategy rather than mere chance.

Indeed, as shown in Figure 2.3, Salesforce is onto something with respect to hiring SDRs with work experience under their belts.

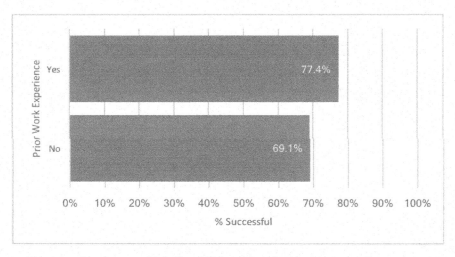

Figure 2.3 Success rate of Salesforce SDRs with and without prior work experience

This means there is a cost of sales tradeoff—while tenured hires are more effective, they are also more expensive. Salesforce appears to have settled on 3 years of experience as the sweet spot for prior work experience, given a median of 34 months and an average of 40 months.

Since medians and averages can mask deeper variation, we further split the success rate by years of tenure as shown in Figure 2.4. Notably, SDRs with less than 1 year of work experience are, on average, less successful than those with more time in the work force.

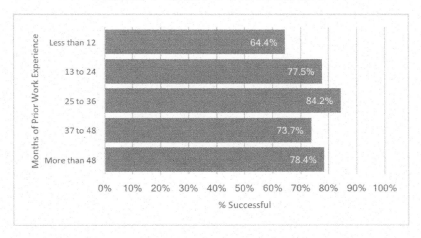

Figure 2.4 Success rate of Salesforce SDRs by years of prior work experience

Does job hopping matter?

Most hiring managers view job hopping, typically defined as spending less than two years in a position, as a red flag. Of course, people do change jobs for positive (ex: better opportunity), neutral (ex: layoffs), and negative (ex: poor performance) reasons. Given this range of reasons, which made us question the validity of the consensus managers view.

To that end, we took the number of months of work experience for each individual after graduating college and before starting at Salesforce and divided it by the number of jobs held during that same period.

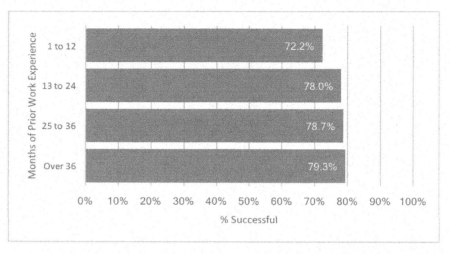

Figure 2.5 Success rate of Salesforce SDRs by average pre-Salesforce job tenure

As we see in Figure 2.5, job hopping is a yellow flag only for tenure less than 12 months. This effect is almost completely due to people with less than 12 months work experience. In fact, people with average job tenure of less than 12 months but more than a year of work experience have a 77.1% success rate as SDRs at Salesforce. Hence, we conclude that worries over job hopping are unfounded and should be ignored.

Does prior industry experience matter?

Now that we have a rule of thumb to target candidates with at least 2 years of work experience, the next logical question we need to ask is, "Which type of work experience is best?"

Conventional wisdom holds that it is best to hire people who possess both industry experience and sales experience. Since such candidates are hard to find, managers take sides on which of the two is more important. Let's look at prior industry experience first.

At least for Salesforce (see Figure 2.6), industry experience matters, but not in the way you might expect. When hiring managers talk about industry experience they mean directly-relevant experience selling

18

similar products to similar personas. Interestingly, people who worked in Salesforce's own sector, technology, fare about average, whereas candidates from professional services thrive.

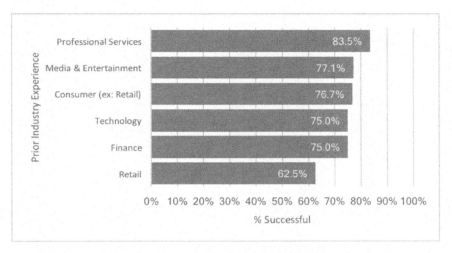

Figure 2.6 Success rate of Salesforce SDRs by prior employer industry

This finding is easy to explain–positioning Salesforce requires a highly consultative approach, just the same sort of approach one would expect people to have learned in the professional services business. SDRs who get promoted to AE at Salesforce often worked in the following professional services sub-segments: major accounting/consulting firms; research & advisory firms, and recruiting firms.

The low success rate for SDRs that come from retail backgrounds mirrors our experience. These jobs have few peaks and many valleys. Employees spend most of their time stocking and tidying shelves; conversations with customers, when they do happen, are generally shallow ("Do you have this in red?") and transactional.

Retailing, we've discovered, may even atrophy the muscles we've identified as critical. While working in a store won't lower GMA or conscientiousness, it rarely puts curiosity and grit to the test. If retailing were about going outside the store and actively pulling people in, then it would be great training; but that is not what it is.

Does prior sales experience matter?

In evaluating SDR success we've challenged the conventional wisdom that prior, directly-applicable industry experience matters. Now, it is time to put theories on prior sales experience to the test, which could certainly be one of the major drivers behind the benefit of hiring people who have worked for least two years after college.

Let's start by looking at where prior sales experience stands in relation to other job functions. Of note, 64% of SDRs hired by Salesforce worked in a sales job function; the remaining 36% are 'career-switchers.'

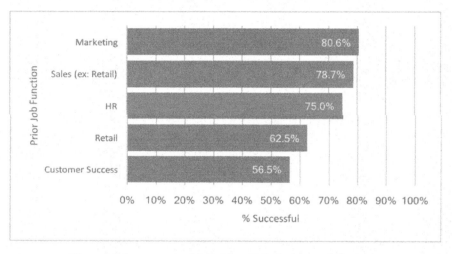

Figure 2.7 Success rate of Salesforce SDRs by prior job function

The findings in Figure 2.7 once again make intuitive sense. Yes, prior sales experience is correlated with success. For Salesforce, marketing experience also makes sense because SDRs with that background know the needs and the language of a key role involved in the buying process.

Many of the people who were in Human Resources job functions prior to joining Salesforce as SDRs were working as recruiters. We too have found this a fruitful source of talent. In addition, though not shown in Figure 2.7 due to low sample counts, we have had success with former teachers and former journalists. Both professions tend to attract 'people-people' who are intelligent, curious, and conscientious. As a bonus, they tend to have strong verbal and written communication skills.

Former entrepreneurs also tend to make great SDRs since they are likely to be strong on grit. We found four hired by Salesforce–one ran a small mortgage company, one formed a group deals site for digital goods, one operated a pet lodge for a decade, and one sold shoes. All four were promoted from SDR to AE at Salesforce. We do not care if their businesses succeeded financially; in fact, they would not have become SDRs if they had.

The jobs with lower success rates similarly withstand investigation. In contrast to working in retail, customer success experience did not impact one's curiosity or grit. However, we found that customer success managers are wired to delight either through nature or training. On the other hand, successful salespeople must create constructive tension rather than working tirelessly to preempt or diffuse it.

Returning to the observation that prior sales experience is correlated with SDR success, be prepared to dive deeper into precisely what sort of sales experience.

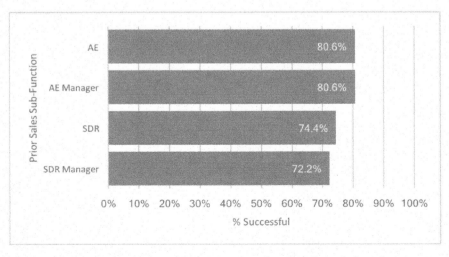

Figure 2.8 Success rate of Salesforce SDRs by prior sales sub-function

As shown in Figure 2.8, former account executives (and AE managers) who move down to SDR when they join Salesforce are more likely to succeed than former SDRs who move laterally when they join the company. Once again, Salesforce seems to be acting intentionally, since 71% of their SDRs here are former AEs and AE managers.

Why would people with AE titles make this sacrifice? We have taken both a pessimistic and an optimistic view. Our pessimistic supposition is that these are people who know they want to pursue a career in sales, but were not succeeding elsewhere; consequently, they decided to take a step back to hone their skills in a world-class environment. Our optimistic hunch, which we actually think is more likely, is that these are people who were working in more transactional selling roles that wanted to move from the minor league to the major league of B2B selling. They were willing to sacrifice title (and possibly pay) to invest in their long-term career. Our optimistic explanation also foots nicely with one of the 'Core Four.' Making such a sacrifice is the very definition of grit–perseverance and passion for long-term goals.

We are both wary of hiring SDRs laterally into our organizations. To even rate consideration, any individual would have to come in through referral and have a history of quantified success. Essentially, they would need to prove their proposed move is because of a significant underlying issue in their organization having nothing to do with their own work.

ACTIVITIES
Does participation in college athletics matter?
Now it is time to look closely at whether sales success is tied to participation in college sports which most managers strongly believe is true. These managers often cite star sellers who were star athletes. It does seem as if there is some logical basis to this conclusion when you consider that successful athletes must have grit in order to win in competitive sports events.

This theory, though, seemed too obvious so we did some serious digging. We started by noting if a person played an official school sport, a club sport, or no sport; we saw no major difference. Next, we checked the specific sport each person played, however the sample size for any given sport was just too small to draw any conclusions.

We finally found the signal in the noise when we classified a sport as individual or team. As shown in Figure 2.9, SDRs who were individual athletes (diving, golf, gymnastics, swimming, tennis, track, etc.) were more likely to succeed. Notably, team sport athletes (baseball, basketball, football, hockey, lacrosse, soccer, volleyball, etc.) were no more likely to succeed than people who did not play sports in college.

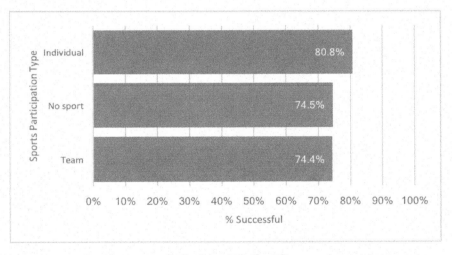

Figure 2.9 Success rate of Salesforce SDRs by college sports participation

Our best explanation for this observation is that sales is a solitary sport. Yes, sellers are supported by teams of people–their manager, sales engineer, operations, etc., but successful prospecting demands eyes-forward, headphones-on solitary focus to grind out 50 or more calls and 50 or more emails, each day every day. SDRs cannot rely on anyone but themselves to pick up the slack and get the work done.

How about other activities besides athletics?

For that, we return to Schmidt's and Hunter's research on job perfor-mance.[8] They found interests predict a mere 1% of the variation in job per-formance. Hence, we do not waste our time on extracurriculars, lest we fall prey to our own confirmation bias.

The Bottom Line

You now have a picture of how to screen resumes for great SDR candidates. Rather than ordering by impact, we feel it is best to order the following criteria by 'frequency' in the reasonable applicant pool:

- Prior work experience: 2+ years

- Immediate prior role:

  o Good: AE or AE manager, recruiter, teacher, journalist, or entrepreneur

  o Suspect: Retail, SDR, or CSM

- College athletics: Individual sport athlete (rare)

- College GPA: 3.5 or higher (very rare)

- College degree: STEM (extremely rare)

You now also know that there is much about an applicant's history that does not contribute toward future success and is best ignored, espe-cially college rank, directly related employer industry, job hopping, and non-sports extracurricular activities.

Having whittled down the stack of resumes using data-driven predic-tors of success, in the next chapter we turn to our approach for systemati-cally interviewing candidates in ways that test our 'Core Four' hiring traits.

CHAPTER 3
Screening Talent by Phone

After rigorously screening resumes according to the data-driven guide-lines in the prior chapter, your next step will be to conduct 30-minute phone interviews with candidates. As with resume screening, we strongly recommend that managers conduct these calls themselves even if a recruiter had introductory conversations with the individuals. The purpose of these calls is to seek out the same Core Four traits–intelligence, curiosity, conscientiousness, and grit—as you did when screening resumes. What's more. this is where you get your first chance to gauge an applicant's verbal communication skills.

Start the conversation with the following three questions that are designed to work together to root out the applicant's motivation to the all-important: "Why now for a career in sales at our company?" This the hiring equivalent of the familiar marketing messaging framework "Why you? Why you now?" (WYWYN).

What do you love about your current role and what has you open to making a change?
Since 30 minutes can fly by quickly, we always start each screening call by saying,

"Thanks so much for taking the time to talk. I just want to confirm that 30 minutes still works for you. (pause for answer). Great, just to let you know, I do have a hard stop." This phrasing conveys that the conversation will be highly focused.

We then transition with the phrase, "Great, let's dive in...." and then continue the conversation by asking the first main question, "What do you love about your current role and what has you open to making a change?" Ordinarily, we do not like being on the asking or receiving end of two-part questions. We made an exception here because we did not want to inadvertently lead candidates into reciting their resumes, but instead wanted to test the extent to which they were running toward being an SDR at our company rather than running away from a bad situation. If they pass this screen this opens the door into digging deeper into their prior roles. Here, however, we are striving to get a sense of what makes this person tick professionally.

The best answers you can hear to this question are along the lines of, "There are such and such great things about my current job, but the organization I'm with does not provide a path to achieve my goal of ___."

Despite the softball nature of this question, many candidates do see an opportunity to unload their frustrations with their job, coworkers, or even the company and its products. When that happens, note that those are all red flags.

What do you love about sales? or for career switchers, "What has you interested in a career in sales?

Recall that for long-term goals grit is perseverance plus passion. Asking "What do you love about sales?" gives you a chance to confirm their understanding of, and passion for, the life for which they are signing up. Moreover, the answer to this second question in combination with the first reveals whether this person is wired for hunting or for farming. Since half of our mission is to create account executives, direct those more suited to the latter towards your customer success team.

Be aware that the delineation between hunter and farmer is often subtle. Almost everyone will state some variation of, "I like to build relationships with people." However, the hunters add, "I like that sales is a place where you control your destiny. where you sink or swim on the measurable basis of your effort and skill, and where what you do has a direct line of sight to the top-line of the business."

Some hunters will go so far as to say they are competitive or money-motivated. When they do, we probe to encourage them to show, not tell us, by asking more probing questions, such as, "Competitive to what end?" "Money-motivated to achieve what goals?" As we stated previously, we need the deeper rationale tied to control of their destiny.

Why (your company name)?

Ask "Why (your company name)?" to test conscientiousness. Generic answers such as "I want to join a high-growth organization" or "I want to be in tech" are not the responses you want to hear. Instead, you want the candidate to demonstrate that they have truly prepared for this interview. What continues to shock us is that some candidates actually expect us to tell them and sell them on the position and on our company--even in a red-hot job market. When you encounter this behavior, it's immediate cause to reject the person.

In contrast, great answers reflect that a person took the time to understand our business. Their knowledge about your company will come across in many forms: from your mission and values to your culture, our products and services, to your career path, and so on. We've learned that the best candidates always go deeper than browsing our website and checking us out on GlassDoor. Motivated candidates, for example, reach out to a current employee or an alumnus to get a real feel for the place. When they talk about what they learned about us, we hear not only their words but feel the passion behind them in the way in which they talk to us about us. After all, if they are unable to show passion during an interview, despite being nervous, then how in the world can they show authentic passion when they call prospects?

CHECKPOINT #1; GO OR NO-GO

It's at this stage of the screening call that you need to quickly reflect on the answers you've heard to these first three questions and make a few important decisions in regard to this applicant.

If we detect too many red flags, we simply open the conversation to a few minutes of questions s a matter of respect for the candidate with the goal of wrapping up the interview in under 20 minutes. Even when we do not feel this person would be a good fit, we want to assure their experience is a positive one because (selflessly) they are people just like us and because (selfishly) we want to prevent negative reviews on job sites like GlassDoor.

Go

If the candidate passes Checkpoint #1, take some time to set expectations starting with the positive aspects of the role at your company. Yes, we are saying you should "tell and sell" but only after establishing their motivations and their conscientiousness.

While we do not have an exact script for this, we often take this opportunity to explain why we joined our organization. Then, we link the growth of our team to the success we have had growing revenue by securing meetings for our AE partners with senior executives at target organizations.

We set expectations by framing the SDR role as an approximately 18-month program split into modules which we describe at a high-level. At SalesLoft, Jeremey's employer, the SDR role has 3 modules tied to achieving cumulative production of 60, 120, and 180 meetings that turn into sales qualified opportunities. An individual becomes eligible for promotion to

AE when they achieve the last milestone. AlphaSense, Alea's employer, has five skills-based modules that are both tied to performance thresholds and provide Sales Development reps increased exposure to and responsibility for different aspects of the sales process from qualification to closing. At both of these companies, people who work smart and work hard earn rapid promotions.

Whether using metrics-based modules or skills-based modules, or a blend of the two, the ultimate mandates remain the same: That the sales development team profitably drives new business for the organization and that the sales development team develops SDRs into successful AEs at our companies. The modules show our disciplined commitment to invest in our new hires by giving them the confidence and the skills they need to go toe-to-toe with AEs who are two to three years more tenured and have not had the benefit of a similarly structured program. (We describe the modules in much more depth in Chapter 7.)

After selling the role (the "what") and the impact of the role on the organization and on their career (the "why"), that we briefly address any questions they have about those topics and before we move on to role-play.

Role-Playing

The question for sales leaders is not if but when and how to role-play with prospective candidates. Since we take nothing as a given, we digress for a moment into whether role-playing is predictive of success in the job.

Fortunately, the answer is yes. We return to Schmidt & Hunter,[9] who focused on intelligence and conscientiousness because those personnel measures are predictive of job success and can be determined by rapid, inexpensive assessments. However, the researchers found (perhaps unexpectedly) work sample tests to be the most valid predictor of job performance, explaining 29% of variation in success.

We held this important information back until now because work sample tests are usually expensive for both candidates and employers. But in sales hiring we are lucky because role-playing is both highly informative and rather inexpensive. This is why we role-play during the screening interview rather than waiting for an on-site interview.

Our strategy is to begin by asking the candidate if they have participated in a sales role-play in the past. Since most of the folks we interview are career switchers, this may be their first exposure and may even be anxiety provoking. We quell any fears they may have by letting them know this is not the first time we have interviewed someone unfamiliar with role-playing, and it will not be the last. Then, we explain the process simple and nonthreatening way, as follows: "I'd like you to pitch <my company> to me. You'll have two to three minutes to garner enough interest that I'm willing to schedule time to continue the conversation." In addition, we assure them that we will walk through the role-play when we finish so they can get a sense of how we sell as well as a sense of us as managers and coaches.

Our choice to have them pitch our company back to us is intentional. As cliché as it sounds, we still hear plenty of examples of "sell me this pen" or similar. A more common alternative is to allow the candidate to choose what they feel comfortable pitching. However, our job as interviewers is not to make applicants comfortable, but rather to assess their abilities. Having them pitch our company to us further tests their conscientious preparation for the interview. That said, we do allow them to choose which persona we play. If they are not familiar enough with whom we sell to, then we choose a role and brief them on the background. We then say, "Take a minute to collect your thoughts. We will start when you say, 'ring-ring.'"

Interview consistency is incredibly important to ensure accurate comparison across candidates. To that end, we always throw out the same three objections. They start with, "Hi, this is <candidate name> calling from <our company>. Is this <interviewer name>?" and we lob our first objection, "Wait, I'm sorry. Where are you calling from?" This is an easy objection to guide them towards while concisely stating our value proposition.

Most people unfamiliar with role playing talk too much and ask too few questions, but we do not ding them for that. We find that perhaps one in four ever asks a question and one in fifty asks layered questions. What is even more predictable is that most ultimately move in for the close with, "Do you want to schedule time so we can talk more about this?" to which we reply with our second objection, "You know, we already work with a lot of <what your company does> today. So, we are not really looking to add another one to the mix, but I appreciate the call." We ten allow for the inevitable and uncomfortable pause to develop.

For those unsinkable creative types who power through the second objection, we float a third one, "Send me an email with an overview of what you do and I'll respond if I'm interested."

The Walk Through

The walk-through is as important just as the role-play because it reveals the candidate's coachability, intelligence, and curiosity. We deliver feedback in two stages. We start by outlining our 6-step call structure, derived from Sandler Training. (See Chapter 11.) Next, we provide build-on/think-about feedback covering strong points and development areas in their role-play. The initial build-on is invariably telling them they did a solid job given a very challenging scenario–pitching our company to us with zero notice. After that, the build-ons and think-abouts are based on precisely what transpired.

Incidentally, by giving feedback by means of this walk through we are setting favorable expectations for what it will be like to work in our organizations. Most candidates get excited because receiving positive feedback was a big part of what was missing in their prior jobs.

The best candidates engage us in constructive discussion, asking questions and actively vocalizing what they are learning. We also love it when they take notes. It is hard to explain every scenario, but as managers you will intuit when a candidate is truly connecting the dots. Mediocre candidates listen politely and do not engage on either our call structure or our suggestions. The worst candidates, though a rarity, are feedback resistant. Since we run feedback-rich teams, we reject candidates who either do not engage or who resist.

To be clear, we are not suggesting you look for a perfect role play from career switchers or even from salespeople with some experience, though you should expect a bit more from the latter. Your goal is to look for conscientious preparation, intelligent objection handling, the grit to rally through a tough scenario, curiosity when receiving feedback, and verbal communication skills demonstrating likeability.

By the same token, you need not search for candidates with flawless diction. The occasional filler word (um, ah, like, you know) is humanizing. Instead, pay more attention to each candidate's underlying sophistication of language and clarity of thought. In other words, ask yourself if you would be willing to put this person on the phone with your most senior target prospects after a modicum of training. If not, reject the candidate.

Questions and Next Steps

After providing role-play feedback, we invite the interviewee to ask questions. A lack of follow up questions for us is an obvious red-flag, and it should be for you, too. The failure to come up with questions suggests a person who is either incurious or uninterested in the role. Conversely, an engaged candidate asks, and we love to hear, questions like, "What makes a person successful as an SDR here at <company name>?" Or they ask about the "day-to-day" responsibilities of the role and about our compensation structure. Truly great people ask, "Based on our conversation, do you have any reservations about hiring me?" followed by "What are the next steps in your hiring process?"

At the end of the interview, be prepared to outline your three-step hiring process. Step one is the phone screen which you've just wrapped up. The next two steps consist of a case study and a set of in-person interviews, topics we explore in the following two chapters. In addition, if you really like the candidate, be sure to let them know immediately that they are moving forward to the next round.

CHAPTER 4

Testing Talent

As we've now shown, knowing how to effectively use both the resume screen and the phone screen will allow you to build a foundational understanding of each candidate's Core Four traits (intelligence, curiosity, conscientiousness, and grit). But as you advance candidates through the hiring process using our process this next step will allow you to add further evidence of these traits and open the door into being able to assess an individual's existing or latent selling skills.

Because every day in the life of an SDR involves researching accounts and prospects, then it's super important that the candidate be adept at engaging contacts through various channels, typically phone, email, and social media. The role-play exercise you've already conducted during the phone screen gives you a sense of an individual's ability to participate in intelligent and articulate conversation with a prospect. But before you commit to investing valuable time in meeting a candidate face-to-face, you need to conduct another work sample test, a case study, to evaluate this candidate's ability to conduct research and to draft personalized emails.

TESTING WRITING SKILLS
Start by giving the candidate the following case study instructions:

The Written Case Study

Please complete the following case study by 6pm on <2 days from now> using whichever format you prefer (Word, PowerPoint, PDF, Google Docs, Google Slides, etc.):

1. *Select a large company and map out their key operating divisions.*

2. *Identify 10 people within one of the operating divisions you identified in Step 1, who would be viable prospects for us. , Provide name, title, and LinkedIn profile URL for each.*

3. *Select one of the 10 prospects you identified in Step 2 and explain why our solutions would be valuable to them.*

4. *Draft the email that you would send to the prospect you identified in Step 3 if you were reaching out to them for the first time on behalf of our company.*

Evaluating the Case Study

Independent of content, the assignment itself provides another test of conscientiousness. Though we do not have exact statistics, we find about 90 percent of candidates complete the case study before the deadline. Of those who do not, about half go dark and half ask for an extension. We eliminate the interviewees who go dark (for obvious reasons). In the rare instances where we did follow up, the person usually ghosted us because they accepted another offer. In those cases we felt as though we dodged a bullet by avoiding a candidate who lacked the grace to exit in a manner without leaving a positive impression. After all, the world of B2B sales is a small community where relationships are important to the job and often built over the span of decades.

While we have granted extensions, we view this as a yellow flag such that the person must truly impress us when they do deliver the assignment. Because we are human, we accept and expect that others have periodic challenges in their lives outside of work. However, we presume that all candidates go the extra mile to put forward the best version of themselves during the interview process. If a candidate requests any type of special treatment, we imagine this pattern will continue as an employee.

Just as we cautioned you not to look for a perfect role-play, the same holds true for expecting a flawless case study. Since interviewees are still in the getting to know us stage, we do not expect they will pick what we feel is the perfect company, division, or target prospect. Instead, we are looking to see if their choices are logical. Sure, it is possible that you might happen upon the great candidate who gets every piece correct. Then, too, plenty of other good candidates might choose an operating division we would not normally sell into and still be able to make the best choice out of the available personas.

With respect to the overall deliverable, we are similarly not looking for visual perfection–we are hiring SDRs not graphic designers. That said, we do expect the interviewee to produce something they would be proud to put in front of a prospect. For example, we expect consistent formatting (e.g., using the same, tasteful font throughout.)

The words matter more and are what we care about since they best reflect conscientiousness and writing ability. Look for work free of typos and grammatical errors. Sentences with language that is direct and concise and light on jargon.

We're not sure if you noticed, but our fourth instruction does not explicitly tell the candidate the purpose of the email; that too is a test. The reason is that we expect the interviewee to clearly position our value proposition and, most importantly, to ask for a meeting.

TESTING INTELLIGENCE

The decision of whether to conduct an intelligence assessment requires careful consideration since such testing is expensive. While the financial cost is not prohibitive, less than $5,000 per year for an organization with 250 employees, the real costs lie in the burden placed on applicants and in the administration and interpretation costs borne by the employer. Jeremey speaks to this issue firsthand as he was required to take an intelligence test for his current role. With only a week of advance notice he purchased and completed practice tests to refresh his skills and get his timing down. Jeremey saw this as a challenge, but some quality candidates might not react in the same way and balk by withdrawing from the process, especially if equally attractive employers do not impose the same burden.

The Personal Interview

In order to avoid the expense of testing some hiring managers may reason they are good judges of intelligence. But how do they truly know? And, moreover, who is to say that candidates can't fake higher intelligence in a job interview?

Professor Nora Murphy of Brandeis University tackled both questions in her doctoral dissertation[10]. She began by administering an IQ test to 182 undergraduate students, finding an average score of 108. Next, Murphy created 91 groups by randomly pairing participants. Each group was then randomly assigned to an Acting or a Control condition. In groups assigned to the Acting condition, one of the participants was randomly designated as the Actor and the other one the Partner. In groups assigned to the Control condition, both participants were given the Partner designation.

In separate rooms, both Actors and Partners were told they "would be interacting with another individual for 5 minutes, during which they would [be videotaped discussing] a preassigned topic." The three randomly assigned topics were living on campus; favorite movies/recently viewed movies; or, high school experiences. Partners were given no additional instructions. Actors, however, were instructed to "impression manage the appearance of intelligence by trying to appear smart, competent, and bright during their interaction." They were also instructed "not to fabricate any information and not to tell their partner about the instructions."

At the end of the 5-minute discussion, each participant rated "how much his or her partner appeared to display three intelligence-related attributes: competent, bright, and smart (each scale 1-9; anchors from not at all to very much)." Since the intercorrelation of the three attributes was high, she combined the items into a composite intelligence score.

Murphy had 56 video judges rate the intelligence of participants. They were unaware of the impression management instructions and simply asked to rate IQ on a scale from 80 to 140. Somewhat interestingly, video judges were fairly accurate in estimating Actor intelligence, but highly inaccurate in assessing Partner intelligence; hence, people attempting to fake higher intelligence do a better job of conveying their actual intelligence than those generally being themselves. More interestingly, video judges did perceive Actors to be more intelligent than Partners.

Murphy found four behaviors correlated with both measured and perceived intelligence: responsiveness; self-assured expression; speaking time (or number of spoken words); and eye-contact while speaking. In addition, she found a number of behaviors correlated with perceived intelligence but not with measured intelligence, including: eye-contact while listening; upright posture; clear, expressive voice; gesturing; nodding; and number of pauses.

Now if we got your hopes up, we will now tear them down. To the dismay of hiring managers, Professor Murphy found "accuracy in perceiving intelligence was not achieved by interaction partners, regardless of impression management" and "Actors were not perceived as more intelligent by the Partners than the controls were perceived by their Partners." In other words, people are not good in one-on-one conversations, at either estimating intelligence or at faking intelligence.

While academic achievement is a strong indicator of cognitive ability, you now know you need something more than unstructured conversational interviews to accurately evaluate intelligence. Before we turn to commercial intelligence assessments, let's look into infamous brain-twister interview questions that can help accomplish the same end.

Puzzles and Brainteasers

Interestingly, Google eliminated this practice as early as 2013, concluding: "On the hiring side, we found that brainteasers are a complete waste of time. How many golf balls can you fit into an airplane? How many gas stations in Manhattan? A complete waste of time. They don't predict anything. They serve primarily to make the interviewer feel smart."[11] However, two years later, the same individual clarified, "Part of the reason is that those are tests of a finite skill, rather than flexible intelligence which is what you actually want to hire for."[12]

Even though the prior quotes from the then SVP of People Operations at Google shared his opinion that brain-teasers did not predict job performance across a range of roles at Google, we, though, are after something more specific–namely, are puzzle questions an effective technique for gauging intelligence? Once again, we turn to academia to find the answer.

Researchers[13] administered an IQ test to 76 participants then videotaped them answering the following five puzzle interview questions:

1. You have a 3-quart bucket, a 5-quart bucket, and an infinite supply of water. How can you measure out exactly 4 quarts?

2. If the United States was interested in reducing the number of states from 50 to 49, which state should be eliminated and why?

3. How many gas stations are in the United States? Please give an estimate and describe how you arrived at your estimate.

4. You have eight billiard balls. One of them is "defective," meaning that it weighs more than the others. How do you tell, using a balance, which ball is defective in two weighings?

5. You have a bucket of jellybeans in three colors–red, green, and blue. With your eyes closed, you have to

reach in the bucket and take out jellybeans. What is the minimum number of jellybeans you can take out to be certain of getting two of the same color?

Interview Scores vs. Puzzle Scores

The researchers found good news, bad news, and worse news. The good news is that the correlation between interview scores and IQ tests was statistically significant and decent by social science standards; more concretely, variation in puzzle interview scores accounted for 20% (R-squared) of the variation in IQ. The bad news is that achieving this result required averaging the scores (on a 1 "poor" to 5 "excellent" scale) of three skilled raters who reviewed the video recordings. That process is simply too complex for SDR hiring (and probably any hiring for that matter). The researchers summarized the worst news as follows, "The moderate correlation indicates, however, that a substantial proportion of the variance in puzzle interview performance is accounted for by other constructs." In lay terms, detecting only 20% of variation in IQ is simply not good enough.

All this leads to the conclusion that an IQ test must be conducted in order to assess the Core Four traits of intelligence. The researchers in both of the studies mentioned in this chapter used the Wonderlic Personnel Test (WPT), a 12-minute, 50-question cognitive ability test with proven[14] reliability and consistency. The nearly identical Criteria Cognitive Aptitude Test (CCAT) has similarly accepted quality.[15] We strongly recommend using one of these tests to assess the general mental ability SDR candidates (but only if one plans to set a go, no-go threshold). Furthermore, we suggest you give candidates one week to take the test so they can adequately prepare.

Testing for Curiosity, Conscientiousness, and Grit

Wonderlic, Criteria Corporation, Devine Group, Predictive Index (PI), and many others offer non-cognitive assessments. Most of these providers test for the "Big 5" personality factors – conscientiousness, neuroticism, extraversion, openness to experience, and agreeableness. Of course, the characteristic we care most about is conscientiousness. Curiosity and grit assessments are harder to come by, though there is at least one provider, Koru[16], that offers both.

Do accept that humans may be as fallible in identifying these three personality traits as they are in detecting intelligence. However, we now avoid subjecting candidates to personality tests after doing so in the past. The problem was that we neither saw hiring managers use the results to filter out candidates nor use them to modify their interview questions. In addition, we feel our approach, inclusive of resume screening, phone screening, work skills testing, intelligence testing, in-person interviewing, and reference checking gives a much stronger sense of each candidate's curiosity, conscientiousness, and grit.

CHAPTER 5

Interviewing Talent

We interview applicants in order to fairly, accurately, and consistently select talent from a candidate pool. We know that sounds relatively straightforward and obvious, but when humans evaluate each other the situation can get notoriously challenging and complicated. As with our previous hiring steps, this chapter shows you how to streamline the process of interviewing and choose the best talent.

Maintaining Fairness

We all like to think of ourselves as fair and unbiased when it comes to judging others—which is, essentially, what takes place when we interview a job candidate. But like it or not, we all harbor unconscious biases that may influence how and why we gravitate toward certain types of individuals and this can work against us when trying to hire the best person for a position. Indeed, a wealth of research[17] backs this up with proof that both conscious and unconscious biases lead to discrimination based on race, ethnicity, national origin, gender, gender orientation, age, physical attractiveness[18], disability and other characteristics. To illustrate how this can play out, consider the following study[19] assessing whether moderately obese individuals would be discriminated against in a mock employment interview.

Researchers filmed one male and one female actor in each of four situations determined by crossing job type (sales representative versus systems analyst) and body type (normal versus overweight). The normal weight female actor (5'6", 142 pounds) was made to appear 170 pounds by a professional makeup artist who used special effects makeup and prosthesis. By similar means, the normal weight male actor (5'8", 5'9") was made to appear 194 pounds.

The scientists also constructed a single job description and resume to be used for each of the two positions. "The information contained in the resumes…dealt with job relevant attributes such as previous experience, education, motivation, and so on." Hence, any potential gender and weight bias were isolated by having one resume and job description for each of the two roles. Moreover, "all applicant materials were piloted and tested to ensure they depicted applicants who possessed average abilities."

Each of the 320 volunteers read one randomly selected job description and resume, watched one video, and then indicated whether they would hire the job applicant by using a 7-point scale, where 1 = definitely not hire and 7= definitely hire. After rating the applicant the volunteer reviewers were asked to assess the applicant's body weight on another 7-point scale, where 1 = underweight and 7 = overweight. This last step validated the effectiveness of the makeup and prosthesis since the actors were rated 6.8 out of 7 when made to look overweight and were rated 3.6 when shown as normal weight.

The data revealed the following:

- Normal weight applicants (mean=5.75) received hiring ratings 36% above overweight applicants (mean=4.22). The researchers added "applicant's body weight explained 34.6% of the variance in the hiring decision and was the most powerful predictor studied in this experiment."

- Male applicants (mean=5.41) received hiring ratings 19% above female applicants (mean=4.55). According to the researchers, "Gender bias against women explained 10.4% of the variance in the hiring decision."

- The bias against being overweight is stronger for females than it is for males. An overweight female (mean=3.61) received hiring ratings 35% lower than her normal weight (mean=5.52) counterpart. Conversely, an overweight male (mean=4.83) received hiring ratings only 19% lower than his normal weight counterpart (mean=5.98).

- Weight bias is not heightened in jobs with extensive public contact (sales jobs) relative to desk jobs (systems analyst).

As we stated earlier, we all like think of ourselves as fair and unbiased and assume the best in people which we hope relegates the source of such biases to the realm of unintentional (unconscious). We both train our interviewers to combat their unintentional biases using Project Implicit® from Harvard University. Tests for weight, gender, and range of other biases can be found at https://implicit.harvard.edu/implicit/takeatest.html.

The Importance of Accuracy and Consistency

Hiring consistently and accurately means that any interviewer (or group of interviewers) would not only hire the same individual from a set of candidates, but also hire the individual most likely to succeed in the role. For this reason we use structured interviews where all applicants are asked the same questions in order to help achieve those dual goals.

In contrast, consider how Schmidt and Hunter[20] describe the opposite interview format: "Unstructured interviews have no fixed format or set of questions to be answered. In fact, the same interviewer often asks different applicants different questions. Nor is there a fixed procedure for scoring responses; in fact, responses to individual questions are usually not scored, and only an overall evaluation (or rating) is given to each applicant, based on summary impressions and judgments." This is such a common practice and the reason that many interviews do not succeed in the choosing of the best candidate that we are willing to bet that most interviews in which you have participated were unstructured.

Again, science backs us up in our assessment of the superiority of structured interviewing. Schmidt and Hunter found structured interviews explain 26% of ultimate variation in job performance whereas unstructured interviews explain only 14%. In fact, it seems that when an interview is combined with an intelligence test, the case for conducting structured interviews is even stronger. Together, structured interviews plus GMA tests explain 40% of variation in job performance, but unstructured interviews plus GMA tests explain only 30%. In other words, you would be wasting both the employees and the candidates' time if you engaged solely in unstructured, in-person interviews. Worse yet, due to the biases we just discussed, you might even leave yourself open to making the worst applicant choices!

The good news is that academia tells us we need to conduct structured interviews whereby each interviewer asks applicants the exact same set of questions, scoring the answers according to a rubric. The not-so-good news is that no one, to our knowledge, has researched the optimal structured interview questions for hiring SDRs.

Constructing Multi-Dimensional Interview Questions

We regularly hear the following words used to describe types of interview questions: behavioral, competency-based, and situational. As there are no universally accepted methods of evaluating the responses these three types of interview questions elicit, maybe because the terms are not clearly defined, we apply the following two-by-two classification framework:

- The first dimension, attribute, includes competencies or behaviors. Think of competencies as job skills or knowledge and think of behaviors as personality traits.

- The second dimension, context, includes historical or situational. Historical focuses on actual events whereas situational focuses on hypothetical events.

Sample Interview Questions

To make this clearer, the following are examples of questions we suggest asking an SDR candidate:

- Historical + Competency-Based: Tell me about a time when you had to sell a product, service, or an idea to someone.

- Historical + Behavioral: Tell me about a time when you… worked on a team with someone with whom you did not get along.

- Situational + Competency-Based: What would you do if… a prospect did not show up for a scheduled discovery call?

- Situational + Behavioral: What would you do if… you disagreed with your manager?

Unpacking the "Science" of Interview-Based Hiring

Without hard science to guide us, our best hypothesis is that asking job-relevant questions is less important than ensuring the right number of qualified interviewers rate candidates on a consistent set of questions. Let's unpack.

For starters, what is the right number of interviewers? Fortunately, Google looked at a subset of five years of hiring data and, "It turns out there is a diminishing return on interviewer feedback. Based on their statistical analysis, the team found that four interviews were enough to predict whether someone should be hired at Google with 86% confidence [see Figure 5-1]. After the fourth interviewer, the increase in accuracy dropped off dramatically—with each additional interview, the accuracy of the mean interview score's ability to predict a hire/no hire decision increased less than one percent."[21]

Increase in accuracy (ability to predict hire/no hire decision) of the mean interview score

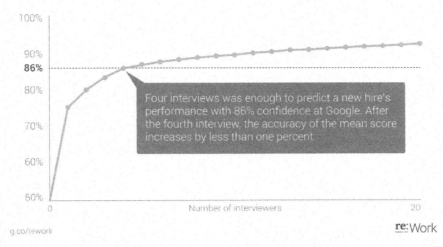

Figure 5-1: Hiring accuracy vs. # of interviewers (Source: Google)

Next, what does it mean for interviewers to be qualified? Google calibrates across interviewers by a process of shadowing and reverse shadowing. With shadowing, an experienced interviewer leads the interview; with reverse shadowing, an interviewer-in-training leads. In either case, the two interviewers need to meet before the interview to review planned questions and to premeditate what great answers sound like. During the interview, the 'shadower' observes quietly but may jump in if needed to steer the interview in another direction. After the interview, the experienced interviewer and new interviewer score the candidate independently and each write notes recording their assessment of the candidate. They compare these assessments only after submitting feedback to an independent hiring committee.

Rating the Candidates

Google rates candidates on a consistent set of questions. The company appears to provide interviewers with considerable leeway crafting questions as long as they assess candidates in four areas:

- General cognitive ability: Demonstrated through problem-solving and decision making (albeit avoiding brainteasers)

- Leadership: Linked to Google's Project Oxygen[22] findings, including, but not limited to, coaching, empowerment; inclusiveness, communication, and results-orientation.

- Job-related knowledge

- Googleyness: Inclusive of collaboration, helpfulness, navigating ambiguity, and "how you push yourself to grow outside of your comfort zone."[23]

From what we have been able to gather[24], each interviewer crafts their own set of questions and their own scoring rubric[25] to judge candidates in the above four areas. This at least ensures a degree of consistency as to how each rater assesses multiple candidates. In addition, the flexibility allows interviews to be conversational rather than robotic.

THE ALPHASENSE ONSITE INTERVIEW AND DECISION PROCESS
Effective Interviewers

Like Google, we pass candidates through four onsite interviews; unlike Google, we do not have legions of interviewers. Instead, in order to ensure consistency, we call upon the same four people every time– our Vice President of Sales Development, an existing SDR, an account executive, and our Chief Revenue Officer (CRO).

Each of our interviewers has a track record of successfully identifying talent. Our existing SDR interviewer is successful in the role, though not be the top-performer, and this person need not be. What is most important is that this person in this role be genuinely interested in interviewing people and have their finger on the pulse of the team in a way that allows them to educate the candidate, to assess culture add, and to vet whether the person can do the job. Our AE interviewer started their sales career as an SDR and is a proactive partner to the Sales Development program – heavily invested in SDR talent development outside of the interview process. In addition to depth of knowledge, their mere presence shows that we truly walk-the-walk in developing talent. Our CRO plays the long game; he knows today's SDRs are tomorrow's AEs, managers, and hopefully, our future senior sales leadership.

Talent-vetting skill is not the only criteria we use to choose interviewers and it should not be for you, either. Be mindful in selecting a set of people who accurately reflect the diversity of your culture. For example, we pride ourselves not only on diversity of protected characteristics like race, color, gender, sexual orientation and so on, but also on diversity of personal and professional experience. We put our culture out front because we want candidates to be able to make an informed decision if they want to work with us.

The first interview is with our Vice President of Sales Development who, schedule permitting, conducts a 45-minute interview. She starts by framing expectations for the day–the people with whom the candidate will meet and the purpose of each of those discussions.

The candidate's interview with the existing SDR serves three purposes.

First, we want the interviewee to get a sense of what the day-to-day experience is like working in the role at our company. Since we hire many career changers, we want them to fully understand the environment they are entering and role they will inhabit. Being an SDR means spending 18 months, give or take, relentlessly researching and engaging prospects who rarely respond.

Second, we want candidates to vet our leadership with someone currently on the team; yes, we want each candidate to understand the strengths and development areas of the person who will be their manager as well as our senior leadership team. We do this because a big part of employee engagement for new hires is all about avoiding surprises.

Third, we want the existing SDR to assess whether the candidate can do the job and is a culture-add. We expect our AE to assess the interviewee's intelligence and curiosity and they do this by previewing our two-way 'service-level-agreement.' Specifically, our SDRs deliver meetings with high-quality prospects in exchange for feedback on where and how to prospect as well as coaching on skills to help the SDR achieve their promotion to AE. Our AE also works closely with the Sales Development and senior leadership teams so is able to provide an addition perspective on vetting our leadership with the candidate. Keep in mind that the AE needs to be focused on assessing intelligence and curiosity and to that end it's not just the answers to the questions but the engagement of the candidate that counts in this heightened area of evaluation.

Our CRO uses the TopGrading[26] interview format to assess grit by understanding each interviewee's personal and professional life story. Companies that use this format have been shown to reduce their mis-hire rate by 85%.[27] During a TopGrading interview, we ask the candidate to step through their resume in chronological order. For each job, we repeatedly ask the following questions:

- Why did you accept this role?
- What were your targets?
- What where your successes?
- What were your failures?
- Who was your boss? What where his/her strengths and weaknesses?
- In this role, what would your boss say where your strengths and weaknesses?
- Why did you leave?

In addition, our CRO sells candidates on us by sharing the importance of our sales development team to the achieve our revenue growth goal. Finally, we use this interview to assess the candidate's existing or latent ability to hold a conversation with a senior executive since that is exactly the persona they will engage if we select them for the job.

Our Vice President of Sales Development frames all of this in less than ten minutes. Having already thoroughly vetted the candidate during the intensive phone screen, she then simply opens the floor for the interviewee to ask questions. She watches how candidates regain composure after the uncomfortable realization that they will need to drive the conversation for the next 35 minutes. Fortunately, nearly all interviewees have prepared a set of questions for the day; it is a huge red-flag (lack of conscientiousness) if they have not. Good questions include "We talked briefly about your training program, can you please go deeper on that?", "How many people on your team advance from SDR to AE?", and "What is the culture really like here at AlphaSense?" We consider it an important green flag when candidates ask questions reflecting they researched our Vice President of Sales Development, since that speaks to their ability to do the job.

Like Google, we allow each interviewer to craft their own questions to facilitate conversation rather than mechanical interrogation. That said, as described above, each person has a well-defined role to play. To recap, our existing SDR vets culture add and ability to do the job, our AE vets intelligence and curiosity, and our CRO vets grit. Moreover, we achieve consistency by having the same team interview each candidate. We gather regularly to share interviewing best practices (ex: Ask historical + competency-based questions that begin, "Tell me about a time when you...") and to calibrate, especially when we disagree on candidates.

As we mentioned previously, Google puts hiring decisions in the hands of an independent committee which reviews feedback submitted by interviewers. While we accept that may be the scientifically best way to do things, we follow the traditional approach of allowing the hiring manager to make the ultimate decision.

Our applicant tracking system (ATS) requires interviewers to provide a final recommendation of strong yes, yes, maybe, no, or strong no. If the hiring manager is not a yes or a strong yes, then we pass on the candidate. Importantly, our CRO, no matter how much he likes a candidate, will never override the manager's decision to reject them. (We have worked with some leaders who reserve the right to reject a candidate they do not like – a reasonable rule. While our CRO will not override the manager's decision to reject, they do reserve the right to override the manager's decision to hire if they've had an extremely negative experience.)

If the remaining four interviewers are also yeses or strong yeses, then the decision to hire the candidate is easy. Things are a bit more subtle when one or more others come back with a maybe, a no, or a strong no. In such cases, the hiring manager reviews the feedback they submitted to the ATS and then speaks with the interviewer(s) directly. For instance, we recently had a candidate where the AE recorded a maybe. When we spoke with him, he said, "I'm not a no. But, I'm not strong yes either because I thought the candidate's eye contact could have been stronger." We extended an offer because neither the hiring manager nor our CRO or existing SDR had that experience.

At AlphaSense, we conduct candidate-supplied and backchannel reference checks for all sales roles except SDRs. For early career professionals, we have found candidate supplied references rarely have a deep understanding of a candidate's skills and are always glowing in their praise of the person's personality. Similarly, backchannel references are very hard to come by; the best references are people the interviewee has worked for, yet we risk 'outing' their intention to change employers.

The SalesLoft Onsite Interview and Decision Process

SalesLoft's SDR hiring process is quite like AlphaSense's. Nonetheless, we will highlight a few differences in approach. For starters, SalesLoft has three rather than four interviews with candidates when they come onsite.

SalesLoft's chief revenue officer does not meet with candidates; instead, the hiring manager conducts the TopGrading interview. Following the discussion, the manager rates the applicant on: (a) consistently grows and adds value; (b) more company-centered than self-centered; (c) not a job hopper; (d) push versus pull into new jobs; and (e) receptive to constructive criticism.

During the peer interview with an existing SDR, we ask the interviewer to assess the following: (a) likes to learn new things; (b) listening skills; (c) meets technical requirements; (d) receptive to constructive criticism; (e) relationship-building skills; and (f) tech-savvy.

The third interview with SalesLoft is a culture fit interview which is often, but not necessarily, conducted by an AE. At the time of this writing, SalesLoft has a 4.9 out of 5 rating on GlassDoor[28]. One unsolicited employee review says, "I have NEVER worked in an environment where a company's core values lasted beyond the onboarding packet." This interview is a critical means by which we protect and enhance our culture. Interviewers rate candidates on the following five core values: (1) bias toward action; (2) focus on results, not merely tasks; (3) glass half full; (4) puts customers first; (5) team over self.

The second minor difference relative to AlphaSense is that SalesLoft uses Google-like 'certified interviewers' rather than the same team every time. The main reason for the difference is simply that the SalesLoft SDR team is at least two times larger than the AlphaSense team. All people involved in hiring candidates at SalesLoft must train on our approach and calibrate to ensure consistency and fairness.

The final difference is that SalesLoft does reference check SDRs by contacting individuals supplied by the candidate. Like AlphaSense, we do not pursue more intensive back-channel reference checks for SDRs.

PART II

SETTING YOUR TEAM UP FOR SUCCESS

CHAPTER 6
Compensating Talent

This chapter provides a step-by-step guide to sales development compensation planning, but before we get there we would be remiss if we didn't first address the even bigger question that has been kicking around the zeitgeist, "Does variable compensation drive performance?" According to author Daniel Pink, who concluded in his 2009 bestseller, DRIVE, "Our current business operating system–which is built around external [extrinsic], carrot-and-stick motivators–doesn't work and often does harm. We need… [a] new approach [that] has three essential [intrinsic] elements: (1) Autonomy – the desire to direct our own lives; (2) Mastery–the urge to get better at something that matters; and (3) Purpose–the yearning to do what we do in the service of something larger than ourselves."

When CEOs, CFOs, and even chief revenue officers read Pink's advice they began to question the effectiveness of traditional variable compensation plans for sales professionals. We believe Mr. Pink intended to position the relationship between intrinsic motivation and extrinsic motivation as an AND rather than an OR; the author simply wanted to highlight an opportunity to increase the focus on intrinsic motivation for knowledge workers. Yes, people will work better and harder when jobs are designed to provide autonomy, mastery, and purpose. And, yes, people will work harder and better for more money.

Five years after Drive was published, a group of academics gathered 183 studies spanning 40 years comprising 212,468 participants.[29] This is what they discovered:

- In the absence of extrinsic motivation, intrinsic motivation explains 7.3% of variation in performance.

- In experiments that include directly relevant extrinsic incentives, intrinsic motivation explains 9% of variation in performance. Hence, extrinsic motivation interacts with intrinsic motivation in a way that actually amplifies the effect intrinsic motivation has on performance.

- Together, extrinsic motivation and intrinsic motivation explain 18% of the variation in performance. Reconciling this with the numbers above, 7.3% of variation in performance is explained by intrinsic motivation alone, 1.7% is explained by the presence of both types of motivation, and 9.0% of the variation in performance is explained by extrinsic incentives.

- Extrinsic incentives have a more powerful impact on quantity of performance, whereas intrinsic motivation has a more powerful impact on quality of performance.

Again, using science as our guide, we will stick with variable compensation plans for salespeople while striving to design jobs and build cultures that offer autonomy, mastery, and purpose.

Now, on to the promised step-by-step compensation guide.

A GUIDE TO SALES DEVELOPMENT COMPENSATION PLANNING

Step 1: Determine on-target earnings (OTE)

OTE is total cash compensation, inclusive of base salary plus variable commission, paid at 100% quota attainment.

Start by understanding the local market benchmark since national averages can be highly misleading. If you do not have access to premium salary benchmark data, utilize GlassDoor to look up salary information. Table 6.1 shows average salaries for the job title "Sales Development Representative" on GlassDoor in several major U.S. metropolitan areas.

Area	Base ($)	Variable ($)	OTE ($)	Mix (%)
Atlanta	49,906	17,747	64,653	73/27
Austin	48,582	18,254	66,836	73/27
Boston	55,198	20,496	75,694	73/27
Chicago	52,357	19,572	71,929	73/27
Denver	45,053	17,145	62,198	72/28
New York City	59,807	22,107	81,914	73/27
Portland	47,876	18,058	65,934	73/27
Salt Lake City	49,114	18,490	67,604	73/27
San Francisco	62,484	24,691	87,175	72/28

Table 6.1: SDR Compensation by Major Metropolitan Area[30]

Due to high variability, we caution leaders to avoid national average SDR compensation metrics. Instead, we suggest adjusting up or down from the local area average based on these five factors:

1. Prior experience: Candidates with strong academic pedigrees or longer prior work experience will expect higher OTE.

2. Job complexity: The more complex the job function, the higher the OTE. For instance, SDRs who conduct discovery calls will expect higher OTE compared to those who primarily book meetings. Similarly, outbound SDRs tend to earn more than inbound SDRs since it requires more skill to engage less receptive prospects.

3. Product complexity and price: This is a special subset of job complexity for SDRs. Engaging customers to discuss expensive, complex products requires a greater level of skill and commands higher OTE.

4. Intrinsic benefits: If you have strong intrinsic benefits--a great brand, a strong culture, an outstanding training program, clear career progression-then you may be able to get away with paying lower OTE.

5. Target attrition: Even with the best product and the most inspiring culture, companies that want lower attrition will need to pay above average OTE. Place higher importance on low attrition when hiring costs and training costs are high.

To facilitate a number of our calculations in this chapter, we use an example OTE of $70,000 which is just above the median of the data in Table 6.1.

Step 2: Choose the target pay mix

The target pay mix is the percentage split of OTE between base and variable compensation. The benchmark average (see Table 1) appears to be 73/27. We frequently see the following: 60/40, 65/35, 70/30, and 75/25; with rare mixes of 50/50 and 80/20; and extremely rare base percentages below 50% or above 80%.

Pay mixes skewed toward a higher variable percentage tend to attract more aggressive, risk-loving candidates. You may characterize this sales personality as a "Hunter." Roles offering more certain higher base compensation are quickly filled, as most humans value low risk/high reward opportunities.

If you are in the early stages of building out your sales development function, then select a higher base percentage because at this stage you do not yet have good data and can easily end up either underpaying or overpaying.

To continue our example, imagine we split the $70,000 OTE as $50,000 base and $20,000 variable, or 71/29 percentage mix.

Step 3: Select variable performance measures

Since we are about to delve into a lot of detail, it's important to give you the bottom-line-up-front: For most organizations, we recommend paying on 70% of variable compensation on opportunities created and 30% of variable compensation on ARR from closed-won deals.

Consider the simplified sales funnel shown in Figure 6.1. An SDR engages in a cadence of activities, including phone calls, emails, social touches, etc. These activities, when effective, lead to a booked discovery (or demo) meeting. If the meeting is held and the prospect is deemed qualified, then an opportunity is created. Assuming the stars align, an AE wins the business.

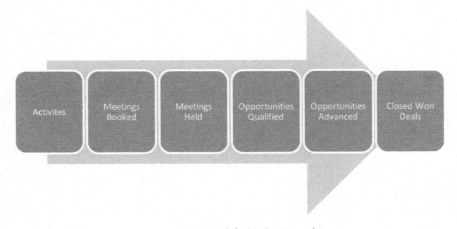

Figure 6.1: Simplified Sales Funnel

Let's now explore the implications of tying compensation metrics to each of the stages in the funnel.

Activities: We do not recommend paying on activities. While activity volume is almost completely within an SDR's control, few companies use activity as a pay metric because (a) paying on activity volume prioritizes quantity over quality; (b) activities are too far removed from business results; and (c) activities are relatively easy to game. If an SDR's job required almost no skill then it would be suitable to pay on activities. It might also make sense to pay on activity volume while an SDR is ramping up, but even that practice is very uncommon.

Meetings Booked: We also do not recommend paying on meetings booked. Paying on meetings booked results in SDRs losing the incentive to do what is necessary to ensure prospects attend meetings. Without best practices in place, 20% to 30% of prospects will be no-show. With the proper reminders, including rescheduling, the percentage of prospects who go completely dark will be closer to 8%-12%.

Meetings Held: Meetings held is the first reasonable metric to consider for variable compensation. If SDRs are given accounts and contacts, pay them up to 100% of variable compensation on meetings held. This keeps them engaged when they lack control over what will happen downstream. If they are given accounts, but are responsible for sourcing their own contacts, then it is a judgment call whether or not to pay on meetings held. If they are given neither accounts nor contacts, then do not pay on meetings held as it creates too much incentive to inject garbage into the pipeline.

Opportunities Created: Opportunities created, also known as sales qualified leads (SQLs), sales accepted leads (SALs), or sales qualified opportunities (SQOs), is by far the most common SDR variable compensation metric. It represents a healthy balance between the company's performance and what is controllable by the SDR.

Opportunities Advanced: If you link SDR pay to opportunities, we recommend linking only to opportunities created and marked as qualified by an AE following the first meeting. Tying some or part of compensation to opportunity advancement beyond this stage is a non-starter. This practice demoralizes SDRs since they don't have control over opportunity progression. Moreover, only small numbers of opportunities generated by a given SDR advance during any given month. Therefore, you'd have set a low quota which would expose the company to uncomfortably wide swings in compensation.

Pipeline Dollars Generated: Pipeline dollars generated (not shown in Figure 6.1) is closely related to opportunities created or advanced. We would only consider paying a percentage of pipeline dollars generated if four conditions are met: (1) SDRs have almost no discretion on expected deal size, (2) AEs have limited discretion on expected deal size, (3) AEs consistently and rigorously qualify SDR-generated opportunities, and (4) the sales cycle is much longer than the variable compensation measurement period. Since these conditions are rarely all present and require a high degree of discipline, we generally do not recommend paying on pipeline dollars generated. Of note, AlphaSense does pay SDRs on pipeline generated due to the length of their sales cycle whereas SalesLoft pays on closed-won deals.

Closed-Won Deals: We recommend paying part of variable compensation on closed-won business–often in the neighborhood of 1.0% to 1.5% of annual recurring revenue (ARR). Paying on ARR aligns SDR pay with company performance and creates strong incentives for SDRs to focus on "good" prospects. Just be aware when going into this that paying a percentage of ARR carries the following problems:

- SDRs have very little control over opportunities after AEs take over.

- With typical 3- to 6-month (or longer) B2B sales cycles, there is an extended gap between activity and reward. This gap not only lowers incentive-driven motivation but also complicates compensation management.

- Two SDRs might get paid very differently for the same work because one SDR had the "luck of the draw." Meaning, one was given a better account or handed an opportunity to a better AE.

At SalesLoft, we once *thought* we had a clever way to give SDRs skin-in-the-game without the aforementioned problems. For two months we pooled 1.25% of ARR and distributed 'shares' based on each SDR's portion of total opportunities created. We acknowledged and accepted the fact that new SDRs benefit from the earlier work of more tenured SDRs (and even from SDRs promoted into new roles). Our rationale was that tenured SDRs got to benefit from this when they were new, so all was fair. In addition, we were excited about fostering more teamwork and dramatically simplifying compensation management.

So, why did we abandon this approach after just two months? Our SDRs figured out they could game the system by generating more opportunities. While that sounds good on paper, more is not always better. The additional opportunities were lower quality with costly impacts down-funnel. In addition, our SDRs unilaterally said the satisfaction of "keeping what they killed" was more important to them than the income-smoothing provided by the experimental plan.

Step 4: Set quotas

Set quotas assuming you chose to include these two measures in your plan: opportunities created and ARR from closed-won deals. Let's begin with examining opportunities created.

The benchmark average quota is 12 opportunities created per month by outbound SDRs selling solutions with an ARR of $25K-$75K[31]. However, the same report this benchmark is drawn from reveals "only 48% of SDRs are consistently hitting quota." [32] From these two data points, we conclude that either SDR performance is not up to snuff or quotas are set too high. While there is always room for performance improvement, we contend that opportunity production is reasonably well optimized. Consequently, the goal must be to set quota such that a target percentage of SDR hit or exceed quota. But at what percentage?

The common rule-of-thumb is that you want 70 percent of SDRs (or any sales professionals for that matter) to meet or exceed quota. You have probably noticed we tend to question most accepted rules-of-thumb in this book, but this one we agree with for two reasons.

The first reason ties into motivation. Imagine the ends of the achievement spectrum. If no SDRs achieved quota then motivation would be low—so low in fact that the team would leave for greener pastures. If 100% of SDRs achieved quota then motivation would also be low. If that last statement sounded counter-intuitive because if quotas were low, wouldn't SDRs maintain or even increase effort to earn additional compensation? Well, don't rush to conclusions.

Even though you might think this to be the case, we find SDRs downshift as soon as they hit quota, even in the presence of significant accelerators. This is because overachievement in one period leads to underachievement in the next. Just like AEs pulling deals forward, SDRs can do the same with opportunities but pay the price later. Benchmark data, shown in Table 6.2, supports our observation; only 12% of SDRs achieve over 110% of quota.[33] Based on our experience, even 50% quota attainment is too low. Think about it: half the people on a team are demoralized every month and cannot help but spread negativity.

Quota Achievement	% of SDR Attaining on a Monthly Basis
Below 50%	9%
50% to 70%	17%
70% to 90%	26%
90% to 110%	36%
Above 110%	12%

Table 6.2: SDR Team Quota Achievement

The second reason we agree with the 70% target attainment rule of thumb is that it aligns management interests and SDR interests. To illustrate, we need to do a bit of math.

We start by figuring out how many opportunities SDR create on average per month. To do that, we multiply the quota achievement row in Table 6.2 by the benchmark quota of 12.[34] Next, we take that result and multiply by the percent of SDRs attaining each level of achievement. Summing the result gives average opportunity production of 10 per month. But this is still not quite the right target quota number.

We want to set the highest target percentage possible so that over-performance of those who meet and exceed quota will balance the underperformance of those who do not. To get there, recognize the performance distribution in Table 6.2 is roughly normal.[35] And, we just discovered the average (or mean) is 10 opportunities created per month. We will spare you the details, but a standard deviation of 3.9 ensures 10% have less than 50% quota attainment and 10% have over 110% quota attainment – just like in Table 6.2. Given a normal distribution, a mean of 10, and a standard deviation of 3.9, setting a target of 8 opportunities created per SDR per month ensures 70% of SDRs meet or exceed quota and the team will average 10.

If all that math was just a little too complicated, here is a simpler approach. If you have enough data, then just set the quota to 80% of the average number of opportunities created per SDR per month. (A big benefit of using your opportunity creation average is that you'll have already accounted for seasonality, vacation, common illness, etc.).

An advanced consideration is what to do during SDR ramp. The most common approach is to make no adjustment during ramp-up; SDRs simply earn less money because they are being 'compensated' with training. The second most common approach is a non-recoverable draw. This simply means SDRs earn, at minimum, their target variable compensation during the ramp-up period. In our ongoing example, this would be $1,667 per month ($20K divided by 12 month). Non-recoverable means SDRs do not have to pay back the commission they were advanced. All other approaches are rare.

However, if you don't have enough data set your opportunity creation quota for outbound SDRs to 8 per month. Adjust the target upward if you sell to small-and-medium sized businesses (SMB) or if SDRs handle inbound lead flow. Adjust the target downward if you sell to large enterprises or to a limited number of personas in each organization.

Now that you have the opportunity created quota, move on to calculating the ARR quota target as follows. The quota of 8 opportunities created per SDR per month means their annual quota is 96. Multiplying this by the benchmark close rate[36] of 22% yields 21 closed-won deals. Finally, multiplying this by an ARR, say $30K, yields an ARR target quota of $630,000.

Recall our example SDR has a $20,000 variable compensation target of which 70% is based on opportunities created and 30% is based on ARR. Hence, the implied payout per opportunity is $145 ($20K times 70% divided by 96 is technically $145.83, but compensation plans are more effective with easy-to-remember dollar numbers). We determine percentage payout on ARR in similar fashion to be 1% ($20K times 30% divided by $630K).

Step 5: Set thresholds and accelerators

Most companies want to limit compensation for underperformers and ramp it up for overperformers. Thresholds and accelerators, respectively, accomplish those goals. Moreover, exposing SDRs to these components early in their careers gives them time to acclimate to compensation structures they will experience as AEs.

A threshold is a minimum performance level, below which no commissions are paid. A common threshold is 40% to 50% of quota. So, continuing our example, if quota is eight qualified opportunities per month, then a threshold of 4 would be appropriate. If you have good data, set the threshold at the bottom 10th or 20th performance percentile depending on how aggressively you want to weed out people. In short, we do not recommend thresholds as they are highly dispiriting. Missing quota that badly is a big enough threat to an SDR's job security that leadership need not pour salt in the wound.

Accelerators are wise because they drive performance and reward for over-performance. The math behind choosing accelerators is all about knowing your desired SDR compensation cost of sale (CCOS).

Let's say that each SDR, on average, is ultimately responsible for creating opportunities that lead to $630K in closed-won ARR. With a $70K OTE, their CCOS is 11%. Building on the example above, the $630K in ARR came from 96 opportunities. The implied value per opportunity is $630K/96 = $6,562.50. Hence, you could maintain the 10% CCOS by paying $656 per opportunity over target.

However, most organizations (and their investors) want their CCOS to decrease as revenues increase. The $656 is a ceiling. The floor is the $145 SDRs earned up until quota. Anything in between is fair. We typically see a 25% to 50% accelerator per qualified opportunity over target. In our example, that would mean paying $180 to $215 per qualified opportunity over target.

Side note: SDRs often find it motivating to know how much revenue each call generates for the company. Assume an SDR makes 300 dials per week or 14,400 per year. If that generates $630K of ARR, then each call is worth almost $44 to the business!

Step 6: Set the performance period and payout frequency

The performance period is the term over which you measure performance to quota. For SDRs, monthly and quarterly are common. Such short performance periods are appropriate for SDRs since their results (meetings and opportunities) follow shortly after their activities.

It isn't necessary that payout frequency match the performance period, but it usually does. If you have a monthly performance period, it makes sense to adopt a monthly payout frequency.

Step 7: Pre-budget for SPIFs

Most sales development organizations run periodic SPIFs (special performance incentive funds) to drive short-term behavior. However, we find few organizations allocate budget for such programs in advance. Consequently, every SPIF requires negotiation with the finance department. To avoid time delays and save energy we recommend pre-budgeting approximately 2% of total sales development compensation cost for SPIFs; this amount should be on top of OTE, not part of it.

Compensating SDR Managers

SDR manager compensation should be tightly aligned with SDR compensation. As shown in Table 6.3, the SDR manager mix is commonly 75/25; first line managers generally have slightly less at-risk than their direct reports. In addition, the variable compensation components should be identical.

Area	Base ($)	Variable ($)	OTE ($)	Mix (%)
Atlanta	64,967	23,027	87,994	74/26
Austin	65,629	23,209	88,838	74/26
Boston	71,908	25,459	97,367	74/26
Chicago	76,856	23,871	100,727	76/24
Denver	67,651	23,834	91,485	74/26
New York City	73,038	25,499	98,537	74/26
Portland	68,477	24,012	92,489	74/26
Salt Lake City	63,354	22,561	85,915	74/26
San Francisco	98,161	32,778	130,939	75/25

Table 6.3: SDR Manager Compensation by Major Metropolitan Area[37]

The SDR manager's quota should be the roll-up of the quotas of their direct reports with a buffer such that SDRs are slightly over-subscribed. For instance, if a manager has eight SDRs each with a quota of twelve opportunities per month, then the roll-up is 96 opportunities. A buffer of 10% is common so the manager's quota would be 87.

A Final Thought

There is an ever-present tension between what SDRs want to be paid for (activities) and what the business wants to pay for (money in the bank). When designing compensation plans, repeatedly ask yourself these two questions: (1) What is simple? (2) What is fair?

CHAPTER 7

Developing Talent

As we mentioned throughout this book, world-class sales development programs must achieve a dual goal of both driving profitable pipeline for the organization and transforming SDRs into amazing future account executives over the course of twelve to twenty-four months. Now that you have a solid understanding of how to accomplish the former, it is time to delve into what will help you successfully achieve the latter goal of developing talent. The best way to do this is by dividing the sales development 'experience' into six modules. Because sales is a meritocracy, we caution you to keep an eye out for those individuals who bring their intelligence and drive to bear since they will become promotion eligible earlier than those who do not.

The six modules are explained below and need to be followed in order as they are progressive in the sense that as SDRs gain the opportunity to develop new responsibilities they must continue to achieve performance metrics. SDRs graduate to the next module when they have not only mastered new skills but also reached clear business performance thresholds.

SIX MODULES FOR DEVELOPING SALES DEVELOPMENT EXPERIENCE

Module 1: Ramping

Module 1 provides foundational skill-building to enable SDRs to consistently achieve the ongoing performance metrics for sales accepted leads[38] (SALs) and pipeline generated. Based on industry benchmarks[39], a good starting point for a ramped SDR is 10 SALs[40] and $250,000 of pipeline[41] created per month.

Key SDR responsibilities during Module 1 include:

- Aligning with AEs on account strategy (i.e. which accounts to engage and which contact personas to engage within those accounts)

- Researching accounts and contacts to identify key business initiatives (especially those who can support with our products and services)

- Adding target contacts to CRM with a high degree of data integrity

- Executing personalized, multi-touch, multi-channel (phone, email, and social) sales engagement cadences

- Conducting light qualification with detailed notes added to CRM

- Scheduling discovery/demo meetings for AEs

- Joining one discovery/demo meeting per week

During discovery/demo meetings held during Module 1, the SDR 'controls' the first part of the meeting inclusive of rapport/introductions as well as the up-front contract. As a reminder, up-front contracts are a Sandler Training methodology that includes meeting duration ("Does 30 minutes still work? Do you have a hard stop just in case we need to cover over?"); your agenda ("Today, we will ask you a few questions to align and then demo the product based on your answers."); their agenda ("In addition, what else would you like to cover today?"; and next steps ("Assuming you see a fit, the usual next step after this call is… I'll pause with about 5 minutes left to see if that is how you'd like to proceed.") After handling the up-front contract, the SDR turns the meeting over to the account executive but stays on the line to listen and learn how to sell.

Expect Module 1 to take an average of 3 months. However, instead of relying on time, we find that setting graduation performance thresholds of 2.5 times the SAL and pipeline targets work best. Using the aforementioned benchmarks, this equates to 25 SALs and $625K of pipeline generated. (Note: We use 2.5x instead of 3x since SDRs 'lose' about 2 weeks in onboarding.)

Module 2: Partnering

In Module 2, SDRs are expected to continue achieving the ramped performance metrics set in Module 1. In addition, they maintain the same responsibilities with one enhancement-- they co-lead discovery with the AE rather than handing discovery/demo calls off to an AE immediately after the up-front contract.

AEs, however, are naturally reluctant to give up control and therefore you need to set guidelines to dissuade AEs from preventing SDRs from participating more deeply in the meeting. For starters, limit the volume – SDRs only participate in one discovery/demo meeting per week. Additionally, AEs need to uphold their end of a service-level-agreement to maintain SDR coverage. Finally, require SDRs hold pre-call planning meetings with AEs to share knowledge and to role-play the coming meeting. For the role play, we expect, as should you, SDRs to develop personalized expressions of our value proposition and to practice addressing expected questions or objections. Notably, SDRs must organize and lead the pre-call planning meeting in a way to provides insight and comfort to the AE; if the SDR fails to do so, then the SDRs loses the right to co-lead the meeting.

We use strong language when describing guidelines that comprise our AE:SDR service-level-agreement. However, we caution you not to create the impression that the relationship is adversarial in any way; far from it. In fact, the goal is to ensure AEs and SDRs are equal partners, what we refer to as "equal business stature[42]." In Module 2, SDRs need to up their game with respect to the level of strategic thinking they bring to bear during pre-call planning. In return, AEs have the responsibility to coach and mentor SDRs to grow them into amazing future AEs.

To give them perspective, we say to our SDRs, "Wind the clock forward a few months when you'll be an AE. You'll have your own sales development partner. What would you want that SDR to do to give you comfort that they're going add value do the discovery/demo call?"

We have also found that it helps to give SDRs examples of what bad and good pre-call planning sounds like. Bad sounds like: "Hey, I just spoke with John Smith. He mentioned this one thing… and I mentioned this other thing…That's about all I know." Good sounds like: "I spoke with John Smith. He shared these two things… Based on what I know about Company X, where John works, it seems like these are some of the strategic priorities… John works on the strategy team and based on some of our other calls with strategy leaders, I'm thinking we probably want to customize the value prop in this way… We probably want to ask these questions…"

Accountability, too, is a thread that runs through everything done to develop SDRs. At other organizations it's not uncommon to hear SDRs say, "We don't get enough training." In our companies we set the expectation early on– even during the hiring process–that SDRs own their own professional development. Yes, even though we are fully committed to formal training we also know full well that SDRs learn more on-the-job then they ever will in a classroom. Every call, every email, every social touch, every interaction with a fellow SDR, every 1:1 with their manager, every pre-call planning meeting, and every discovery/demo meeting is a learning opportunity is a learning experience that should be fully exploited as such. We do our best to instill the fact that the individuals who goes in with a learning mindset will learn and those who go in with a task-completion mindset will stagnate and suffer.

The pre-call planning meeting is an excellent opportunity for SDRs to learn to be thought partners to AEs. We all know that it's impossible to just 'show up' and pull that off, especially as a relatively new SDR. Indeed, conscientious SDRs ensure success by preparing through researching the prospect, the prospect's company, the way to position the product, and the approach for addressing questions and objections.

Expect Module 2 to take and average of 2.5 months. Based on benchmarks, this equates to a cumulative total of 50 SALs and $1.25M of pipeline generated.

Module 3: Positioning

Performance metrics remain the same in Module 3 as in the prior two modules and this aims to give SDRs even deeper exposure to the sales process. While many organizations wrestle with whether to allow trails, many organizations find that trails increase win rates. Hence, SDRs in Module 3 also participate in two additional meetings per week--the kickoff meeting and the success check-in meeting--the bookends of the trail process.

Unlike during discovery/demo meetings, SDRs remain in listen-only mode when attending trial meetings. We give SDRs access to call recordings, but we find that giving them the opportunity to join live calls has a greater impact on learning. This is because they are doing much more than simply listening to any random trail kick-off or check-in call, instead they must focus their attention on joining calls for opportunities they recently sourced. Listening to live calls also gives SDRs the valuable ability to informally engage the AE afterward with questions about the AE's approach. As it is our intent to strive to build feedback-rich organizations we expect SDRs to give as much, if not more, feedback than they receive.

Expect Module 3 to take, you guessed it, an average of 2.5 months. Continuing our example, this equates to a cumulative total of 75 SALs and $1.875M of pipeline generated.

Module 4: Closing

In Module 4, performance metrics remain the same but SDRs gain the right to join one negotiation/close meeting per week. That means that each week the SDR is expected to leads the first part of one discovery/demo meeting, join one trial kick-off call and one trial check-in call, and listen-in on one negotiation/close call. Before and/or after most of these calls, allow the SDR to pre-brief or debrief with their AE partner.

The benefit of doing all of this is that the SDR gains tremendous exposure to the key client conversations that are happening throughout the entire sales process. This is proven out when our SDRs are promoted to AE and ramp at hyper-speed as compared to SDRs who 'merely' source opportunities, get promoted, and only then receive training on the rest of the sales process.

Expect Module 4, like the prior modules, to take 2.5 months. By using the same benchmarks, this equates to a cumulative total of 100 SALs and $2.5M of pipeline generated. Total average time elapsed in role is now 10.5 months.

Modules 5 and 6: Polishing

The preceding four modules are illustrative of our core philosophy of increasing SDR exposure to what they will need to be able to function successfully as AEs. We either allow SDRs to lead parts of the sales process or to participate in listen-and-learn mode, depending on the risk to our business.

We will not go into the details of our final two modules here since they are rooted in our sales processes and not readily generalizable to other organizations. Suffice it to say, though, that the performance metrics and expected time in module remain the same. Hence, the average cumulative time to completion for Modules 5 and 6 is 13 months and 15.5 months, respectively. By using the benchmarks expect that at the end of module 6, SDRs must have sourced 150 SALs and at least $3.25M in pipeline to be eligible for promotion to AE. You should, of course, adjust the numbers based on the economics of your business and the desired time to promotion for the average SDR.

Compensation

You may have noticed that we did not discuss compensation adjustments for SDRs as they advance through modules and this is because compensation depends on your approach to hiring SDRs.

If you hire more senior SDRs, those with 2 or more years of work experience, then the higher on-target earning paid means you need not adjust compensation along way.

If, on the other hand, you hire SDRs with less work experience, then we recommend increasing base salary along the way. CFOs usually strongly suggest adjusting variable compensation rather than base salary. However, sales development leaders need to respond by arguing strongly that not only do SDRs carry lower risk to the organization as they progress, but it is far easier for SDRs and for finance to pay the same amount to every person for any metrics achieved.

CHAPTER 8
Onboarding Talent

From an overarching perspective, the leadership team has an obligation to set new hires up for success by building out the systems that allow them to thrive.

One of the easiest but more important things we do is onboard salespeople in groups. Unless your company is growing at a supersonic pace, we recommend a monthly onboarding cadence. Groups, or "classes," should include sales development representatives as well all other new sales team members since the learning around company/culture, market, products, processes and tools, and sales fundamentals are universally valuable. Moreover, associates learn not only from trainers but also from each other. Most importantly, combining SDRs and account executives fosters collaborative relationships from day one.

While we strongly support the role of sales enablement in architecting the onboarding program and in running some modules, we recruit sales leaders and peer masterminds to run most sessions. We anoint individuals as masterminds when they achieve expert level proficiency on any tool, process, knowledge-domain, or skill area. A true testament to whether the systems you put in place are working is if individuals who have gone through those systems are knowledgeable enough and bought-in enough to train on an ongoing basis. In addition, they bring their in-the-trenches experience to update best practices with what is working in the field.

ONBOARDING SCHEDULE
Week 1

Onboarding should be a two-to-three-week process depending on how long each sales development representative needs to achieve their certifications. During week one, you need to focus learning spans in the areas of: company/culture, market, and product.

Hiring for culture fit might seem like a good start, but we find that deeply indoctrinating new hires is crucial for enabling a faster start and for fostering longer-term associate retention and growth. Rather than simply telling your founders' story, it's much better to have your founders tell their own story, if possible. In addition, bring senior leaders or influential associates from each department to have conversations about how they work with and for the sales development team. We eschew talking through reporting structure (who works for whom) in order to echo that we are a flat organization with a bias toward action and a focus on vision. For example, our Head of Product talks about our artificial intelligence roadmap. Our Head of Marketing discusses upcoming demand generation programs. And so on., Every new hire should know both what they are expected to get and to give across each functional area as a result of participating in these sessions.

During the first week we also focus on educating SDRs on the markets we sell into. Yes, markets is a broad term inclusive of industries and personas and for this reason we lean on account executives and account managers to dissect industries during these sessions. For example, at AlphaSense we target Financial Services as well as large corporations across Healthcare, Industrial Manufacturing, and Technology. In order to effectively dissect an industry an account executive would start with an overview of the industry through the lens of key macro-trends affecting businesses, for better or worse.

It is in that context that they dive into specific product use cases for specific personas. Product use cases should not be abstract, so we ensure account executives are armed with recent value stories of our clients. Each story is meant to demonstrate each use case for our product rather than simply talking through slides. It is through these real-life examples that we can effectively highlight available collateral and still remain focused on helping new hires connect our product to the value customers derive. To further dwell on the importance of this point, we'd like to add that feature-focused onboarding is a major reason salespeople fall into the mode of feature-based selling. To combat this, it's critical that we always make sure to walk-the-walk on value-centric messaging.

AlphaSense embeds a competitive overview as part of the industry and persona sessions. We ethically collect competitive intelligence from several sources, including from several individuals who have worked for several key competitors. These individuals are long-removed from those companies and abide by non-disclosure requirements but are still able to offer incredible perspective on market dynamics.

Above, we mentioned our focus on group onboarding which begs the question, Is collaborative learning superior to individual learning? The science says the combination of "group rewards and individual accountability are held to be essential to the instructional effectiveness of cooperative learning methods."[43] To that end, we inform SDRs on Day 1 that they will be required to present what they have learned about industries and personas back to their peers, immediate manager, and other leaders across the organization by the end of the week. This assignment forces an intentionality and focus to their learning. Questions include: What are the key industries we sell into in the corporate markets business? What are the personas we sell into in each industry? Why do clients in specific roles plus industry combinations choose to buy from us? People who merely take a test after training are rationally involved, whereas people who must present to peers and leaders are emotionally engaged–and even more engaged when they know what questions they are required to answer during the presentation.

Feeding information through the firehose, we also expose new hires to our product during the first week by giving them, you guessed it, a second assignment--with two parts. Abstractly (since we want to avoid even the semblance of self-promotion in this book), AlphaSense is an AI-driven "vertical search" platform clients use to quickly and efficiently find information they might otherwise miss. Part one of the assignment requires new hires to answer several deep research questions about market trends without the aid of our platform. Part two provides each of them with an AlphaSense login as well as a quick functional demo, again with an hour to repeat the task. Unsurprisingly, they struggle in part one and succeed in part two. We find that this "before and after" exercise is one of the best ways to give sellers firsthand experience of the challenges and pain our prospects face in gathering information across disparate sources in a reasonable amount of time.

Following the completion of this assignment, we go deep on product with a series of walkthroughs and demos led by a product specialist delving into features and functionality, including an introduction to our application of artificial intelligence. To make this knowledge resonate, new hires then shadow product specialists for half-a-day to be able to hear firsthand some of the nuanced questions asked by prospects. After the product-specialist experience, SDRs then meet with top account executives who conduct demos linking those features to value-driven use cases.

In order to reinforce an understanding of how we link solutions to customer value, we give SDRs access to our conversational intelligence platform where the call recordings our account executives, account managers, SDRs, and product specialists hold with clients and prospects is stored. The archive is tagged by industry, persona, and use case, so new hires can hear how prospects describe themselves and their challenges, how we articulate our value proposition, and how we address questions and common objections.

Week 2

As SDRs transition into week two of onboarding, it is time to shift focus to certifying them on demo and then cold calls. We suggest holding demo certification first because understanding your product is a precursor to conducting an effective cold call. To round out demo-readiness, continue in-depth product training focused on use cases by industry and by job role.

Take certifications very seriously since SDRs are the tip-of-the-spear in driving business and more than likely the first individuals that prospects will encounter from your company. In our company we ensure quality and consistency with a set of approved certifiers. At present these certifiers include our head of customer success and a veteran product specialist. Either can conduct the assessment by filling out a scorecard with a yes/no grading scale to eliminate ambiguity. Select questions include: Is the SDR able to articulate our value proposition? Are they able to distinguish how we are differentiated in the market? Did they connect features to use cases and value?

We also demo certify all SDRs in a single day and make sure that is accomplished by scheduling the first round in the morning. Those who did not pass in the morning get a second try in the afternoon. Though rarely necessary, this leaves time to retry with waves of certification attempts and feedback into the evening for those who do not pass on the morning try, though most do. Either way, we provide extensive feedback.

After SDRs pass their demo certifications we transition them into discovery and sales fundamentals, relying heavily on Sandler methodologies. Our three favorites are the up-front contract, negative reverse selling (aka "behind the pendulum" selling), and the concept of equal business stature. Our in-house introduction is reinforced by our Sandler instructor[44] who runs training sessions once a month.

OUR THREE FAVORITE SANDLER FUNDAMENTALS

Though it is not our intent to steal too much of Sandler's thunder, we would be remiss without including a least a high-level explanation of our three favorites referenced above.

The Upfront Contract

This framework consists of a rapport (pattern interrupt" for a cold call), time, your agenda, their agenda, and next steps. We've chosen to go with the example for a cold call:

- Rapport/Pattern Interrupt: "Hi, this is Alea from AlphaSense. How have you been?" [The point of a pattern interrupt is to say something tactful but unexpected rather than the same things every other salesperson say such as "Did I catch you at a good/bad time?" We expect that the prospect answers by saying, "I'm sorry, do I know you?" in response to the example above. That response is actually perfect because it shows that they are engaged.]

- Time: "I'll just take three and a half minutes of your time to…"

- Your agenda: "The reason for my call is…share how AlphaSense can help you [relevant value proposition] so that you can decide whether we might be a fit to help your team."

- Their agenda: Though this is usually skipped in a cold call, in a scheduled call we would ask, "In addition to those topics [i.e. the ones from your agenda], what else would you like to discuss?"

- Next steps: "If you decide we might be a fit, we can schedule time to discuss AlphaSense further at a time that is more convenient for you."

Negative Reverse (behind the pendulum) Selling)

To explain the next Sandler fundamental think of a prospect as a pendulum swinging back and forth from right (uninterested) to left (interested). When a salesperson is doing their job well, the prospect's own conviction provides the momentum to the left (interest). The salesperson can follow this momentum closely behind the pendulum but need not be pushy and try to get too close to the prospect. For SDRs, saying "Frankly, I'm not sure if we are a fit for you" is a classic example of negative reverse selling. This is in stark contrast to many SDRs whose pushiness ends up destroying rather than building trust.

Equal Business Stature

We expect through sharing this Sandler fundamental with SDRs that they communicate with prospects as peers. Surely, SDRs do not have the breadth and depth of experience that a CxO has, however, SDRs do understand our solution and our ways of creating value better than the CxOs they call on. Our goal is to provide them with confidence, not cockiness.

It is during week two that new hires complete a DISC[45] assessment which starts with SDRs understanding their personality profile. After which we open the aperture to help them identify and engage with every personality profile to give them perspective. We are careful to stress that no specific personality is better or worse for either salespeople or prospects; rather that each personality has different ways in which they like, often subconsciously, to be communicated with. For instance, Alea is a "D" meaning she is results-driven and likes to get right to the point. Jeremey is a "C" meaning he craves knowledge and process and likes to dive into details. Even though these profiles are generalizations, we find them to be effective starting points.

During a recent session, one SDR said, "I think I get it. Let's say we're planning a trip to a museum. The Ds say 'We should go to the museum. Here are the reasons why... Are we all agreed?' The Is then respond, 'Oh, isn't this awesome? This is going to be such a great trip!' The Ss will ask,

'Is there a cafeteria that can accommodate everyone's food preferences? ' Finally, the Cs will get started planning the itinerary for the trip.

It's important to understand that even a person's initial reaction to an SDRs first words on a cold call provide insight into a prospect's personality profile. The Ds have a pointed, direct, and brief response so we need to get down to discussing value and results as quickly as possible. In contrast, the Is will be more friendly, the Ss more guarded, and the Cs more likely to ask a clarifying question. The communication styles of each of these personality profile types is also reflected in an individual's email response as well.

With Sandler fundamentals in place, we continue to progress in the second week to discovery (cold) call certification by having new SDRs join the daily role-play blocks our captains run with the existing team. We have the new folks observe for one day and then expect them to participate by the second session. During scheduled meetings and unscheduled time, SDRs also role-play with their peers, team captain, and manager to facilitate them in making steady progress in a feedback rich environment.

Though we provide sample value propositions, which we sometimes refer to as "commercials", to SDRs we do not expect them to memorize and regurgitate scripts. A major goal of repeated role-play is to allow the SDRs the opportunity to develop their own language and tone when describing what we do and how to help specific personas. It is interesting how a prospect can quickly detect authenticity and inauthenticity in a representative" voice and this role play helps them hone the way they present themselves and the company. We apply this philosophy to all aspects of prospect engagement inclusive of objection handling, answers to common questions, setting next steps, and so on.

Once a team manager or team captain judges an SDR to be "certification-ready," the new hire attempts to certify with our Director of Sales Development. We impose this two-level system since discovery call certification is our means of clearing new hires to engage prospects via phone, email, and social channels. As with demo certification, if an SDR does not pass on the first try, it is important to repeat these techniques with waves of practice and feedback. These iterations not only develop the selling ability of our SDRs, but also develop the coaching ability of our leaders.

The Importance of Coaching Your Team

You have no doubt noticed the repeated mention of coaching. This is because we feel a strong duty to build feedback-rich cultures on our teams and more broadly in our organizations. What's more, it is our obligation to provide highly specific build-on ("continue") and think-about ("start" or "stop") guidance, a method we refer to as "BO-TA," (pronounced bow-tah). Therefore, it is not alright for a manager to simply say, "Your up-front contract was great." Instead, we expect more detailed feedback. For instance, a better managerial response is, "Let's dive into your up-front contract. Your pattern interrupt was appropriate given the prospect persona in this scenario was a "D." However, you need to be more precise about the expected next steps. If you did it again, how would you frame the next steps?"

For many new hires, this may be the first time they have ever received deep and direct constructive feedback. This means that it may be especially unsettling to some individuals coming from their manager during the first few weeks on the job. This is why we find it critical to set their expectations. We let SDRs know that we will be giving constant feedback in order to help them learn and grow. You may also remember that we also shared this style of feedback during the interview process as a glimpse into our feedback-rich culture and also to assess coachability. Moreover, the feedback we are proud to provide is intended to challenge ideas and skills, not them personally. After all, we would not have hired them after such a rigorous screening and selection process if we did not believe in them and what they were capable of doing. In order for every one of us to be better than we were yesterday, we must open and welcome to receiving feedback today.

The Keys to Near-Perfect Role Play

The following are the attributes we consider to be the keys to near-perfect role-play when conferring a passing grade for cold call certification with our Director of Sales Development.

- Executive presence on the phone, specifically confident tone/ inflection, limited filler words, and sophisticated, yet jargon-free language

- Clear articulation of our value proposition for the persona they will initially target

- Ability to handle common questions and objections

- Beginner or better proficiency with Sandler fundamentals

Once SDRs have been certified as "fearless on the phone," we move into tools and associated processes. This, of course, includes our tech stack for account identification, contact sourcing, and sales engagement to execute multi-touch, multi-channel cadences. Our SDRs learn to "operate" our sales engagement platform while simultaneously learning how to personalize our email templates.

To help SDRs further understand how their jobs impact the way we run and optimize our business, they attend a CRM-focused session with our revenue operations team. Experienced SDRs supplement this training by showing how they use Salesforce.

Week 3 (and beyond)

With two weeks of intensive training and certification complete, SDRs "hit the phones" by the start of their third week. We want our SDRs prospecting our best accounts so we manage risk by having them start out on less senior contacts. However, they start engaging senior executives in a matter of a few days to a week.

Coincident with going-live, we review a set of expectations with SDRs across three categories: (1) activities and results, (2) workflow, and (3) AE partnership.

ACTIVITIES AND RESULTS: Our SDRs have minimum daily call targets as well as monthly targets for sales qualified opportunity quantity (at SalesLoft) or pipeline (at AlphaSense). Our daily call minimums (50 at AlphaSense and 60 at SalesLoft) hold for ramping and ramped SDRs. Our opportunity and pipeline targets, respectively, ramp to full quota over the course of two months.

WORKFLOW: SDR workflow expectations are centered around time management. For instance, AlphaSense SDRs adhere to the following time blocks for active prospecting: 9:00 to 10:30, 11:00 to 12:30, 2:00 to 3:30, and 4:00 to 5:30. In the ideal, this provides 6 hours of engaged selling time in an 8-hour day, or 75%; this is double the industry benchmark rate of 36%.[46] Sales leaders bear critical responsibility for protecting these SDR time blocks; internal meetings, including 1:1s, are not permitted during these blocks. The only exception allowed during time blocks is joining calls the SDRs schedule with prospects.

Once upon a time we made the mistake of restricting each time block to a specific activity, specifically, calls from 9:00 to 10:30 and emails from 11:00 to 12:30. That approach proved too rigid so we now trust SDRs to engage in the mix of activities prescribed by cadence steps in their sales engagement platform.

AE PARTNERSHIP: An AE:SDR service level agreement (SLA) constitutes the final expectations category. For SDRs, we establish standards for data integrity in Salesforce, inclusive of distilling critical information from calls and emails to help AEs efficiently prepare for calls. At SalesLoft, these fields include:

- Person on the meeting (including role)

- Team type and size

- Sales and marketing tech stack

- The prospect's current sales process

- Why do you [the SDR] think this is a good opportunity?

- Additional notes

The AE:SDR SLA works both ways. AEs are expected to provide SDRs with target account overviews. These overviews are informal at SalesLoft but are formal one-pagers at AlphaSense. The one-pagers include information about past trials (if any), key contacts and their disposition toward AlphaSense, common prospect jargon (i.e. business unit names), and any known strategic initiatives.

While the burden of pre-call planning rests mostly with the SDR, the SLA also demands that AEs conduct post-call reviews with the SDR. Such reviews have the short-term effect of focusing SDRs on the right prospects and the long-term effect of training SDRs on what they will need to do when they get promoted.

After talking through the three categories of expectations, we send a summary email to SDRs. We have also heard that some SDR leaders create printed "contracts" for SDRs to sign and post at their desks. Though we do not follow this practice, we leave it to you to consider if that is culturally appropriate in your organization.

Final Thoughts on Onboarding Talent

The concepts in this chapter provide a starting point 'system' to support the success of sales development teams. Optimizing the system requires both science and art. The science demands picking an initial approach, sticking with it long enough to measure baseline performance, then iterating to optimize results. The art, more subtle yet equally important, requires that sales development leaders give their people creative liberty to experiment. One of our mentors summed up this idea as follows: 'As long as you color everything inside the lines, please color as much outside the lines as you like.'

PART III

ACCELERATING PERFORMANCE

CHAPTER 9

Designing Cadences

Because ninety-seven percent of companies already execute multi-channel, multi-touch cadences[47] we need not provide any motivation to encourage that approach. Instead, we will provide a starter cadence combining conventional benchmarks and known best-practices.

Tuning Outbound Multi-Channel, Multi-Touch Cadences

A good starting point for a B2B outbound prospecting cadence, based on benchmark data, is 16 touches over 21 business days executed as follows:

- 7 Emails

- 8 Dials in which SDRs leave voicemails 3 times

- 2 Social Touches

The magic lies in using data to arrange these touches. To begin, we looked at the optimal wait time between prospecting touches.

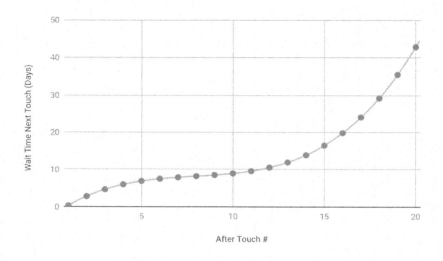

Figure 9.1: Wait time between prospecting touches

Let us explain how to read Figure 9.1: After touch 1, wait less then one day before sending touch 2; after touch 2, wait between 2 and 3 days before sending touch 3; and so on. Rather than try to tune to fractions of a day, we recommend zooming out to clearly see the big picture of what the data illustrates. Specifically, provide breathing room by expanding the time-delay between touches. One hypothesis as to why this approach is effective is based on the fact that humans are wired to ignore regularity. This means that SDRs create a sense of randomness by spreading touches out,. Another hypothesis, by way of metaphor, is that the first touch plants a seed that must be watered over time. Spreading value-added touches over a longish time span allows prospects to respond when they are ready.

The design approach we use is the "+1 rule." Between each touch, add 1 day of delay. Hence, complete touch 1 on day 1, touch 2 on day 2 (+1), touch 3 on day 4 (+2), touch 4 on day 7 (+3), touch 5 on day 8 (+4), etc. For the record, a touch can be a single touch or, the increasingly common, a double touch of phone call followed by email.

Day	Touch A	Touch B	Touch C
1	Research + Social Follow	Call 1 (AM or PM) with voicemail	Email 1
2	Call 2 (AM)	Call 3 (PM)	
4	Call 4 (AM)	Email 2	
5	Social Connect		
7	Call 5 (AM or PM) with voicemail	Email 3	
11	Call 6 (AM)	Call 7 (PM)	Email 4
16	Call 8 (AM or PM) with voicemail	Email 5	Move to nurture

Figure 9.2: Starter outbound prospecting cadence

The starter cadence in Figure 9.2 combines the spirit of the benchmarks and the best practices. Our rationale behind the construction of this cadence is:

Day 1: In order to prepare for a conversation in the happy event of connecting, the SDR starts with research–typically on LinkedIn and the company's website. Since the SDR is already on the prospect's profile, we recommend a social follow, though not yet a connection request. With the research top-of-mind, the SDR executes Call 1, leaving a voicemail if the prospect does not pick up. After the voicemail (our data shows one should call then email), a personalized Email 1 should be sent.

Day 2: Waiting one day, the SDR completed two calls on day 2. We don't have the data to prove this conclusively, but we feel strongly that there is such a thing as leaving too many voicemails. Hence, over the course of the cadence, we leave voicemails only at the beginning, middle, and end. The Day 2 calls, therefore, are dials without voicemail.

Day 4: After a two-day pause the SDR completes Call 4, again without voicemail. Email 2 should be a threaded reply. We have found very simple text like "Any thoughts?" or the more direct "Please Advise" are highly effective. The most aggressive "Bump" works but is very bold and can backfire by resulting in a negative reply.

Day 5: The SDR also sends a personalized LinkedIn connection request now that the SDR has some degree of name recognition with the prospect. Careful readers will note that we have violated the +1 rule. We push the social connection to Day 5 rather than pack it into either Day 4 or Day 7.

Day 7: At the midpoint of the cadence the SDR executes a double-touch inclusive of a call with voicemail followed by an email. If you have a large prospect universe then Email 3 need not be personalized, though you should use a persona and industry specific template

Day 11: This is a touch-heavy day with two calls and a voicemail. Email 4 is a threaded reply to email 3, so short and simple text is best.

Day 16: After a call with voicemail and an email move the prospect into nurture mode with the intent of providing a value-added touch once every 30 days. For high value contacts, SDRs should directly execute the nurture cadence. For lower value contacts, the contact may be moved (back) to a marketing automation platform.

In the sample cadence we indicated making certain calls in either the AM or the PM. This is just a suggestion. We are aware that some people advocate calling during certain times, especially before 9am or after 5pm in the prospect's time zone. The reason they offer for this being the e "best" time to call is that gatekeepers are not available to answer the phone. However, the data we looked at does not support this suggestion. The best time to call is... wait for it... NOW! Though the most obvious reason is that any call is better than no call. If an SDR has a call block (or the motivation to call), then they should just do it.

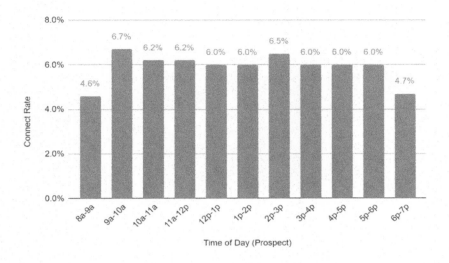

Figure 9.3: Connect rate by time-of-day in prospect's time zone

Figure 9.3 shows the connect rate is around 6% at almost any time of day. And, calling early (8 a.m. - 9 a.m.) or late (6 p.m. - 7 p.m.) is usually worse. This finding makes sense to us because it is during these times that executives are either head-down wrapping up their day, preparing for the next day, or not in the office.

We also considered the best day of week (see Figure 9.4) to send emails and found the same rule applies–the best day to send an email is today. To be more precise, the best day and time is Monday morning between 9 a.m. and 10 a.m. However, most of us do not have the luxury of just sending emails during only one hour per week and then twiddling our thumbs for the other 39 hours of the work week. Moreover, the difference in reply rate between that golden hour and any other hour is minuscule. The only times we would avoid are late Friday afternoon through late Sunday afternoon.

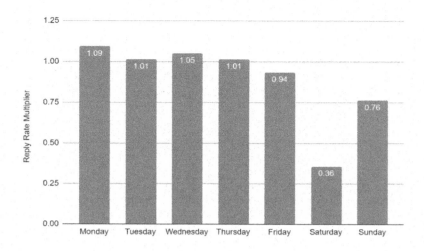

Figure 9.4: Reply rate multiplier by day of week

Responding to Inbound Leads

A lot of old research concerning the response rate to inbound leads is recycled, so we found it more reliable to conduct our own test by submitting demo requests to 100 SaaS technology vendors. As shown in Figure 9.5, roughly 60 percent of companies responded within the currently acceptable window of 1 hour, with 40 percent responding in the first 5 minutes.

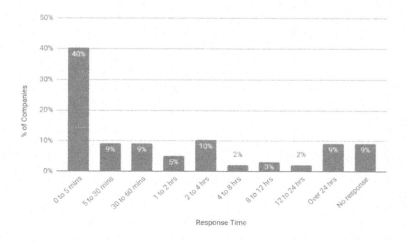

Figure 9.5: Inbound response time for 100 SaaS companies

Since prospects do not always respond, even when they submitted a demo request, it behooves SDRs to execute inbound response cadences. The guidelines we established for outbound cadences apply to inbound responses, except that we recommend dropping the "+1 rule" and executing at least two touches per day for at least 5 days before spreading things out.

Many technologies exist to score and engage inbound leads in well under 5 minutes, including automated email responses with embedded calendars as well as "form-to-phone" solutions. Many companies have supplemented their landing pages with chatbots to speed the inbound routing process, as well.

CHAPTER 10

Crafting Emails

Plenty of valuable content exists outlining what messaging techniques work right now. We equate this to simply "giving you a fish" in the old adage, "Give a person a fish, and you feed them for a day. Teach a person to fish, and you feed them for a lifetime." But that isn't our intent. Instead, we intend to do much more by using this chapter to "teach you how to fish" in order to increase the effectiveness of the SDRs you lead. We will start here with email messaging and then move to multi-touch, multi-channel cadences.

CHOOSING A TEMPLATE

It will come as no surprise that we are diehard adherents of A/B testing, the gist of which, as applied to email optimization, starts with determining your best email template–this is your "A" template. Next, make one small modification in this template it becomes your "B" template. Then start randomly engaging prospects by using either template variant--a 50/50 mix is typical, but any percentage mix will work. Continue to send emails until one template works to engage clients more effectively than the other—and you have your clear winner!

Most sales engagement software already has built in A/B testing so you do not really need to know the underlying math. But when you to know what is inside the "Black Box" you will have much greater confidence in the results.

To begin, let's define "better." The measure of "better" is when the reply rate for template B exceeds that of template A[48]; otherwise, we stick with A until we come up with a new variation to test. Statistics conveniently provide a formula for comparing two proportions (reply rates) given a certain number of trails of each type (emails sent). The equation is the following:

$$Z = \frac{P_B - P_A}{\sqrt{\widehat{P}\left(1 - \widehat{P}\right)\left(\dfrac{1}{N_B} + \dfrac{1}{N_A}\right)}}$$

$$where\ \widehat{P} = \frac{X_B + X_A}{N_B + N_A}$$

Figure 10.1: Z-score formula for 2 email reply rates

Let's break this down. Z, known as z-score, is a measure of the number of standard deviations the reply rate of template B is above that of template A. The larger the z-score, the more likely B is a winner. The rule of thumb is to conclude B is be better if z is greater than +2. If the z-score is between -2 and +2, then the emails are equally effective. If the z-score is less than -2, then A is overwhelmingly better.

PB is the reply rate for template B and P_A is the reply rate for template A. P_B, in turn, is the number of replies (X_B) divided by the number of emails sent (N_B); ditto for P_A.

Finally, $\widehat{P}$ (pronounced p-hat) is the pooled reply rate, which is simply the sum of all replies to both templates divided by the sum of all emails sent using both templates.

If all this seems a bit daunting, do not despair, just Google "Z Score Calculator for 2 Population Proportions."[49] Then you can simply enter values, click a button, and easily get an answer. For example, imagine a test of two email templates yields the following:

- Template A: 5.6% reply rate after 50 emails sent

- Template B: 5.9% reply rate after 50 emails sent

Entering these results into an online calculator gives:

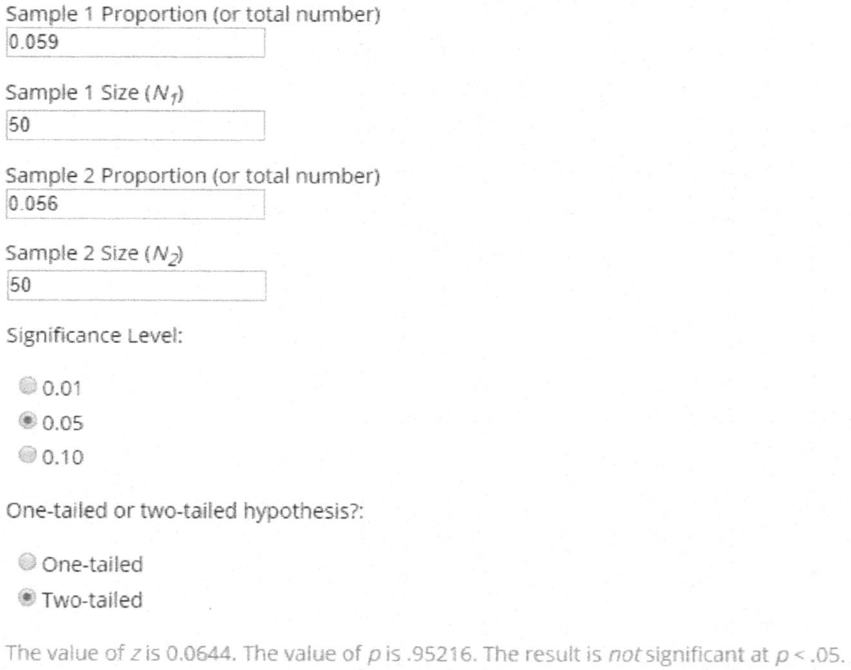

Sample 1 Proportion (or total number)

0.059

Sample 1 Size (N_1)

50

Sample 2 Proportion (or total number)

0.056

Sample 2 Size (N_2)

50

Significance Level:

- ◉ 0.01
- ◉ 0.05
- ◉ 0.10

One-tailed or two-tailed hypothesis?:

- ◉ One-tailed
- ◉ Two-tailed

The value of *z* is 0.0644. The value of *p* is .95216. The result is *not* significant at $p < .05$.

Figure 10.2: Z-score calculator output

From the output, notice the z-score equals 0.0644. Since this is in the range of -2 to +2, we can then conclude that B is no better than A. In other words, given this (relatively small) number, 50 emails of each sent, the 5.9% reply rate is statistically no different than the 5.6% replay rate. Stated yet another way, the 0.3% difference between the reply rates could be random.

If you were to send more of each variant and the reply rates stayed at 5.6% and 5.9%, eventually you could have confidence that the reply rates were different. By analogy, imagine you flip a coin just two times. If you got two heads, you could not yet conclude the coin was unbalanced. However, if you flipped the coin 1,000 times and got heads 900 times, then you would be reasonably certain something was wrong with the coin.

Getting back to our example, just how many of each email would you need to send to conclude 5.9% was better than 5.6%? The answer is just over 48,000 of each. This number is so large because the difference in reply rates is quite small. If B had been 8.9% instead of 5.9%, then you would only need to send about 490 of each.

Now that you have this foundation in how to conduct A/B tests, let's use it to see what to test as either a starting point or as a variant on your existing "A" template.

Unless otherwise noted, the following is based on reply rates to a sample of 5 million emails.

Optimizing E-Mail Subject Lines

Before choosing the actual words you think will work best on email subject lines, you must first optimize the length of the subject line. We chose to keep track of the number of words rather than the number of characters because words are easier to remember and apply. Relative to average reply rates, Figure 10.3 shows the reply rate multiplier versus the number of words in the subject line. Though not shown, subject lines of more than 5 words result in reply rates dropping precipitously below average.

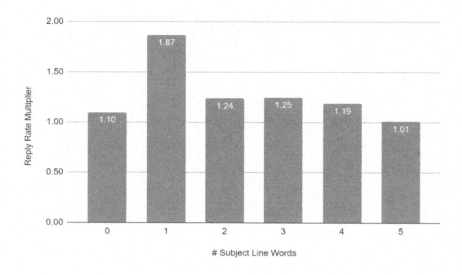

Figure 10.3: Reply rate multiplier vs. # subject line words

Subject lines with only one word commanded the highest reply rates. If you had an average reply rate of 3% across emails of varying subject line lengths, then the data predicts an 87% boost (to 5.6%) by shortening to a single word. Does this multiplier apply to every individual email template? Certainly not; however, the law of large numbers will kick in across multiple campaigns.

When we've shared this data in the past, the question we are always asked is, "What is the magic word?" The good news is there is no one word. Based on samples of millions of subject lines, a great choice is your own company name. We have also seen greetings (ex: "Hey") work along with directness (ex: "meeting"). In case you were wondering, we also looked into using the recipient's first name and company name in the subject line which had a neutral (0.93x) and a negative (0.88x) impact, respectively. These last two worked until the gimmick wore off.

With any such finding, we like to play armchair social psychologist to figure out whether the multipliers will persist over time as many SDRs adopt a particular practice. Those that persist tend to reduce effort; those that fade tend to be pattern interrupts to which prospects grow immune. We believe shorter subject lines will continue to drive higher reply rates.

In contrast, we looked at subject lines written in all lowercase. We imagine there was a time when this was an effective approach since it is unusual at first glance. However, in our sample, the reply rate multiplier for all lowercase subject lines was 0.91x; the loss of nearly 10% is likely due to prospects getting wise to the technique. We imagine the effectiveness of all lowercase subject lines will rise and fade in cycles as prospect immunity waxes and wanes. Rather than try to time the cycles, our advice is simply to always be genuine.

The use of asterisks in the subject line is the counter example to the all-lowercase subject line. When we ran our analysis, subject lines with asterisks carried a 1.88x reply rate multiplier. We suspect this was a case of an unusual, attention-drawing technique that would rapidly shift to having a dampening effect if it became commonplace. As for using other punctuation, exclamation marks were neutral with a 1.06x reply rate multiplier and question marks were destructive with a 0.83x multiplier. We suspect question marks will remain a poor choice for subject lines because they demand immediate effort from prospects.

Being math nerds, we took an in-depth look at the use of various types of numbers. Subject lines that contained numbers have a 0.68x reply rate multiplier; starting with a number is even worse (0.63x). We are not certain why this is, but we suspect that emails with subject lines like "5 tips for driving…" become so ubiquitous as to immediately trigger prospects' mental spam filters. Dollar signs (0.57x) and percentage signs (0.27) are downright disastrous.

Along the same lines, and equally disappointing to us, were subject lines that referenced content or data having lower than average reply rates, or 0.57x and 0.37x, respectively. Also content subject lines that included the words "articles," "info," "tips," "ideas," etc., as well as those that included the words "survey," "benchmark," "analysis," "finding," etc. In these cases, we concede that these emails were designed to deliver value or drive clicks without asking for a reply.

Adding "congrats" (2.00x) or "congratulations" (1.72x), when warranted, boosts reply rates. While using positive trigger events is a fairly well-known best practice, we feel this technique will remain effective because it is very hard for people to resist when their egos are stroked.

We mentioned above that "meeting" is an effective one-word subject line. Even when the word meeting is used with other words, it seems that direct asks boost reply rates by 1.36x. More desirable words in this group include "request," "reconnect," "call," "direction," "introduction," "advice," "talk," "chat," "connect," "help," and "time."

If you have been in sales development for any length of time, you are no doubt familiar with the "break up" email which taps into loss aversion by implying, "If you don't reply now, I'm going away and you'll miss this opportunity." Break-up centric words in subject lines are effective, carrying a 1.3x reply rate multiplier when the following words are used: "adieu," "bugging," "missed," "wrong," "miss," "goodbye," or "bye." (However, don't stoop to the amateurish by asking if the person has been eaten or attacked, accompanied by a picture of an alligator or other predator).

Marketing books love to promote hyperbolic language centered around gains or urgency. However, business-to-business prospects have grown wary of this practice. Gain words ("guaranteed;" "special;" "quick;" "exclusive;" "new;" "free;" "better;" "best;" "revenue;" "value;" "increase;" "offer;" "valuable;" "save;" "savings;" "ROI") have a 0.76x reply rate multiplier. Urgency words are worse still with a 0.71x multiplier ("need;" "limited;" "now;" "ready;" "only;" "last;" "final;" "deadline;" "only"). Avoid gimmicks.

As a general rule, you should craft email subject lines as you would when writing to a colleague inside or outside the company, always avoiding the gain or urgency words, listed above. More generally, we parsed each word out of the 5 million subject lines we looked at and then ran them through a classifier to tag them as positive, neutral, or negative. Subject lines with neutral tones have average reply rates. In contrast, subject lines with a positive tone have a 0.82x reply rate multiplier and those with a negative tone, presumably to provoke or cite a problem, have a 0.66x reply rate multiplier.

The single highest impact word used in a subject line is "referred," which has a whopping 6.36x reply rate multiplier! Of course, the subject line is just the preview to a genuine referral from a close associate of the prospect. If you worked hard enough to get a referral, remember to note that prominently in the subject line.

SUBJECT LINES Dos and DON'Ts

Do:
- Be authentic (no gimmicks)
- Keep them short
- Be direct
- Consider a break-up email
- Use neutral language
- Leverage hard work of referrals by putting "referred" in your subject line

Don't
- Use numbers in a ubiquitous fashion (e.g. 5 tips for…)
- Use hyperbolic gain or urgency language

Never Underestimate the Importance of Your Greeting

If you don't think greetings have much impact on reply rates—think again--they do when all else is equal. One-word greetings like "Jane," for example, have a 0.83x reply rate multiplier compared with two-word greetings which have a neutral impact (1.03x). Among prepended words, "Hey" (1.23x) beats "Hi" (1.01x) which beats "Hello" (0.91x). Our best guess is that "Hey" is at present a friendly surprise, but the benefit will wear off as more sales professionals use it to greet prospects.

We also looked into whether or not to end the greeting with a comma, colon, hyphen, or dash, predicting it would not matter (it shouldn't) and, indeed, it does not.

Fleshing Out the Body of the Email

While we intend to dive into the nuances of optimizing email body text, the most important reply rate accelerator has to do with personalization. But, just how much personalization is sufficient?

One our employers (no names mentioned to avoid any semblance of self-promotion) offers a platform that allows reps to, among other things, send emails from user-defined templates. Looking at 6 million emails, the company calculated what percentage of the starting templates were sent to prospects.

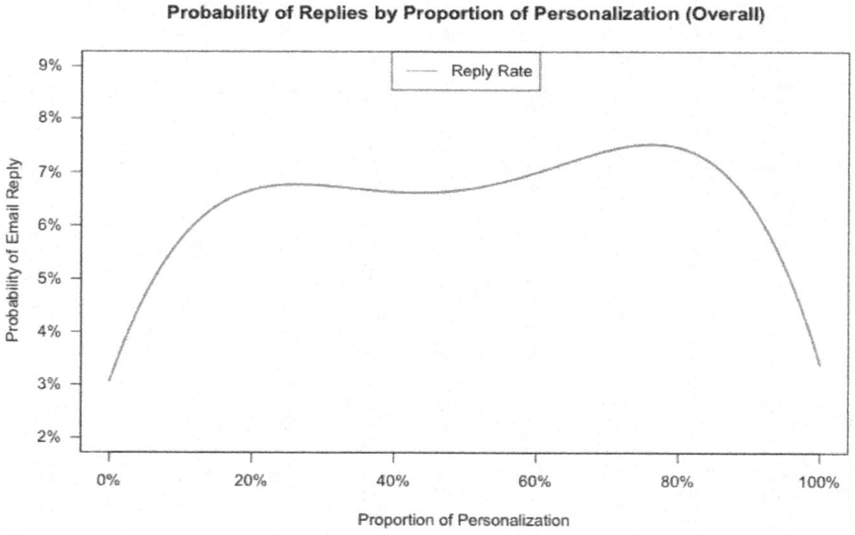

Probability of Replies by Proportion of Personalization (Overall)

Figure 10.4: Email reply rate vs. proportion of personalization

In Figure 10.4, 0% personalization refers to emails where the template was sent as-is. 100% personalization means characterizing situations where reps deleted the template and started from scratch. As shown in the figure, the optimal percentage of personalization is 20%, which is great news since personalization is effortful. However, the research does not say which 20% of the email should be personalized. Our best recommendation is to personalize the first 20%, to show the prospect that you took the time to write to them; we also support the 10-80-10 style of personalizing the first and last 10% of the email. Even if the writing does not touch on other drivers of influence, the fact that a real human took the time to write a real note commands some degree of reciprocity.

If a modicum of personalization helps, why not a lot? Though impossible to know exactly why, our hypothesis is that the email templates reps are given to start with are pretty good. And they should be; after all, the starting template should be the result of continual A/B testing.

OPTIMAL EMAIL LENGTH

Personalization should logically stand the test of time as a reply rate booster. So, too, should the next best practice, optimizing email length.

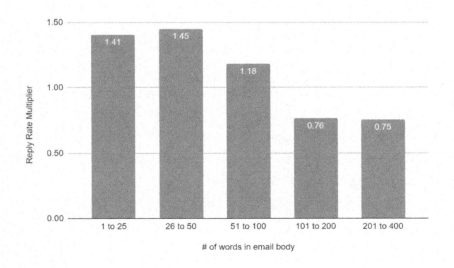

Figure 10.5: Reply rate multiplier versus # of words in email body

Figure 10.5 reveals the sweet spot length of between 26 and 50 words and an upper bound of 100. Especially in this age of shorter attention spans and when many emails are read on mobile devices, we are not at all surprised that shorter is better, though there is such a thing as too short. As illustrated above, anything under 25 words is too short and does not allow the sender to convey enough to optimally engage a prospect. What does 100 words look like? To give you an idea, this paragraph was crafted to be 100 words on the nose.

READABILITY

Next, we looked at the reply rate multiplier as a function of readability. For this, we threw the tens of millions of words from 5 million emails into a Flesch-Kincaid Readability engine and found the following reply rate multipliers were a function of the grade-level of the email copy: Elementary 1.63x, Middle School 1.35x, High school 0.74x, and post-secondary 0.56x. The takeaway–write simply.

Bullets and dashes. We have had some good debates with friends on whether bullets improve win rates. On the affirmative side, the argument is that bullets improve readability, consistent with the prior finding. On the negative side, the counterargument is that bullets have become all too common in generic marketing emails. In the 5 million email sample we looked at, bullets indeed harm reply rates (0.63x). Dashes, likely because they are plain text, are a better choice (0.89x), but skipping either option is better. Note, we did not control for email length when looking at bullets and dashes; hence, the problem may very well be that emails requiring bullets are too long to begin with.

Bullets fall into the family of anything deviating from plain text, all of which are bad. These include underlining (0.87x), **bold** (0.83x), and *italics* (0.76x). We feel these are long-term dampeners since they are the province of spam.

Questions. We turn next to the use of questions in the email body. Recall that questions were harmful to reply rates when used in email subject lines. Fortunately, reps can get away with a one question email body. We recommend using that question for the call-to-action ("Does tomorrow at 2pm work for you?") rather than asking an (annoying) rhetorical question in the main email copy.

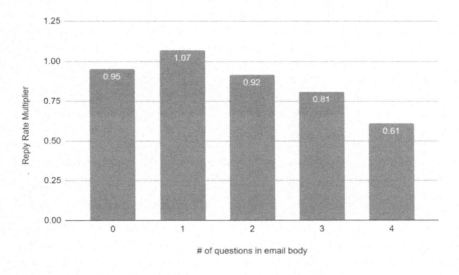

Figure 10.6: Reply rate multiplier versus # of questions in the email body

Links and images. Next, consider links and images. For links, zero is best (1.59x) but one is okay (1.09x); anything over one link makes emails look generic and may trigger the paradox of choice. With images, a single image (1.09x) works better than having no images (0.93x). More images sour quickly. As an example of best-practice, one of the best prospecting emails we ever received had a picture of our own website with modification and annotation related to the seller's product.

Videos. And last, we turn to videos, a subtle topic. No doubt you have seen a video of an SDR holding a whiteboard with the prospect's first name on it. It turns out those do lift reply rates but only when sent in the follow up email and when the video is preceded by about five sentences.

We expect the effectiveness of video emails to decline as the novelty wears off. We can recall watching all such videos when we first started getting them, but we now just treat them like every other email and press delete if not hooked by something else. As we write this, we are seeing reps experimenting with sending video and audio messages via LinkedIn. These early adopters are experiencing strong response rates, but the novelty here, too, will wear off over time.

Content, Structure, and Presentation

The set of best-practices in the prior section are critical at a high-level. Equally valuable, is advice on how to structure and present the email body text so it looks good and is easy to read. We will do that here along with a complementary approach to A/B testing.

We recently decided to test a completely new template rather than A/B incremental changes. To avoid starting from scratch, we stack-ranked on reply rate every email template our SDRs had ever sent more than 500 times. We then parsed the top 10 and bottom 10 templates in the three categories that define most prospecting emails: the hook, the value proposition, and the call-to-action. We were subsequently left with blocks of text that were dominant in the good or the bad templates, as well as language that was no more prevalent in either.

The good, neutral, and poor hooks were as follows:

- Good - Social Proof: "The likes of {{customer 1}}, {{customer 2}}, and over {{number of customers}} all use {{our company}}."

- Neutral:

  o Research: "I was doing some homework on {{prospect company}} and noticed you lead a team responsible for {{responsibility}}."

  o Pleasantries: "I hope this email finds you well."

    ○ Generic introduction – "My name is {{rep first name}} and I work in Sales Development at {{our company}}."

- Poor – Problem/Challenge: "{{Trusted expert}} has found the top challenge facing {{role}} leaders is {{challenge}}."

The good and neutral value propositions (there were no poor ones) were as follows:

- Good - what + why + how: "Keeping it simple, {{our company}} is a platform that combines {{feature 1}}, {{feature 2}}, and {{feature 2}} to ensure {{primary benefit}} by {{primary differentiator}}."

- Neutral – Provocative question: "What are you doing to stand out from the competition?"

The good and neutral calls-to-action, though only marginally different, were as follows:

- Good – Trade time for value: "Are you open to a quick screen share today or {{1 business day from now}} to see how other teams are already {{achieving benefit}}?"

- Neutral – Direct ask: "How does your calendar look for a 10-15 minute chat either today or {{1_business_days_from_now}}?"

What this comes down to is that a good hook should reference social proof. (Later in this chapter we will discuss the use of personalized text to preface or replace the hook.) A good value proposition combines the "what," "how," and "why" of your offering; the order does not matter as long as all three components are incorporated and the statement is direct and succinct. Finally, the call-to-action seemed to be the least critical element; this makes sense, since the hook and the value proposition do the work, leaving the call-to-action as a mere formality.

The Cost and Benefits of Personalizing Email

We have already mentioned that personalizing up to 20% of email content correlates with a nearly 2x increase in reply rates. However, that statistic leaves two critical questions unanswered – Which emails in each cadence should SDRs personalize? What does great personalization look like?

The decision to personalize emails in a cadence is an ROI question at its core. On one side there is the reply rate boost. This is counterbalanced by the opportunity cost of the time it takes to personalize an email.

Let's assume that an average SDR operates at a rate of 60% active selling time[50]; hence, in an 8-hour day, they spend 4.8 hours engaging prospects. Further, assume it takes 10 minutes to personalize an email. Hence, if all they did was personalize emails, then they could personalize 48 per day. The cost, based on $75,000 fully loaded SDR cost per year and 220 working days, is approximately $7 per email.

Now, let's turn to the revenue per email which we will do through four basic assumptions. (update these rates based on your own business):

- R1: reply rate without personalization = 3.5%

- E: engaged prospect-to-opportunity created rate = 10%

- W: opportunity-to-closed won rate = 20%

- A: annual bookings per win = $50,000

Multiplying these four assumptions gives us the expected revenue per email without personalization, $35. Since personalization boosts reply rate by 2x, the incremental and desirable ROI of 5x.

With each successive email, the reply rate drops because interested prospects are more likely to reply early in the cadence. All else being equal, the 'break-even' reply rate is 0.5%. Different assumptions will yield a different decision on which, if any, emails to personalize so it's important to know the metrics for your business and use those in the calculation to make an informed decision.

Simply stated, our general advice is to have the SDRs personalize the first email and automate the rest. That leaves SDRs more time to call prospects. It ia important to note here that this advice assumes you have armed your team with templates customized by account, persona, and industry. Doing this ensures automated emails sent to prospects are suitable. Customization by persona and industry should be considered the minimum viable product of anything your team does–no generic, mass blast emails.

What Great Personalization Looks Like

Another critical concept that needs to be addressed is what great personalization looks like. Years ago, incorporating a prospect's name, company, and/or role was novel and effective. Today, the ubiquity of dynamic tags in marketing automation and sales engagement platforms means such information no longer qualifies as personalization. Genuine personalization needs to create the impression that the SDR invested actual time in learning about the prospect; we may get there in the future, but we suspect machines are still some time away from creating that impression.

Types of Personalization. There are three main categories of personalization: individual, company, industry/role. Fortunately, a research firm[51] conducted a study with 7,000 prospects, varying the subject line and opening text by: industry/role only; company only; individual + industry/role; and individual + company.

In the test, industry/role personalization focused on delivering a relevant insight; for example, the subject line, "The biggest threat to your success in financial services." Company personalization referenced a key takeaway from the prospect company's annual report or press releases; for example, the subject line, "XYZ Bank's brand relaunch strategy." Finally, individual personalization referenced a tidbit from LinkedIn such as, "I see we have a mutual connection on LinkedIn - my VP Mike Miller."

Treatment	Open Rate	Click-Through[52]	Meeting Rate[53]
Industry/role	20.1%	6.0%	3.1%
Individual + Industry/Role	24.5%	5.3%	2.8%
Company	25.2%	5.1%	1.6%
Individual + Company	26.2%	4.8%	1.5%

Figure 10.7: Results of Corporate Vision's Marketing Personalization Study

Figure 10.7 shows the results sorted by meeting rate, the metric that matters most. The strongest meeting rate came from emails with industry/role personalization. The next best is company personalization. While they did not test individual alone, adding this type of personalization negatively impacted the effectiveness of the other types of personalization.

We spoke to the author of the study, Tim Riesterer, to get his hypothesis for what was happening. Tim felt industry/role personalization is effective for two reasons. The first he refers to as the voyeur-effect: people want to know what their peers are doing. That is why benchmarks are in such high demand. The second is the "learning-effect": independent of what others are doing, people crave best-practices.

Tim also has a theory for why company and individual personalization are less effective. For company personalization, the benefit of showing that someone took the time to research is offset by a strong likelihood the prospect is not engaged with the initiative the SDR cited. For individual personalization, plucking a random fact from LinkedIn is perceived as a gimmick. The data suggests this gimmick is negative, not neutral.

Great Personalization - Revisited

You may have noticed the approach to individual personalization in the Corporate Visions study was rather light: "I see we have a mutual connection on LinkedIn…" With that concern in mind, we looked for studies with a much deeper level of personalization but could not locate one. However, we found something amazing in the work of Becc Hoffman and M. Jeffrey

Hoffman. Becc and Jeff don't know each other (yet) but they came to the same insight nearly two decades apart.

To set context, let's start with the common prospecting email shown in Figure 10.8.

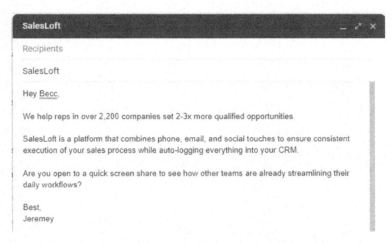

Figure 10.8: A well-optimized but generic prospecting email

The email is well-optimized in the following ways:

- Length: The email is short and sweet – just 56 words.

- Subject: SalesLoft data science has found that 1-word subject lines have the highest reply rates. Moreover, one should use sender's company name in the subject line rather than the prospect's first name or company name.

- Salutation: SalesLoft data science has also found that "Hey" outperforms "Hi," "Hello," or the prospect's name alone.

- Hook (paragraph 1): We looked at SalesLoft's best & worst performing templates. Those combining social proof with positive business impact performed best. Those framing problems or challenges performed worst.

- Value Prop (paragraph 2): Using the same best/worst approach, we found WHAT ("... platform ...") + HOW ("... to ensure consistent execution...") language was most effective.

- Call-To-Action (paragraph 3): The best/worst analysis showed variations in CTA wording have relatively little impact on the reply rate. We like this one because it offers value and implies that this won't just be a painful discovery call.

After running this email for a while, we used more data science (cosine similarity) to check the reply rate versus the amount of personalization our SDRs were applying. We found personalization of at least 20% of email content yielded a nearly 2x increase in reply rate.

Everyone knows they should personalize. However, people are hungry for how to personalize. This is where Becc, building on Jeff's work, steps in with the following premises (ranked from most to least effective):

1. Prospect-created content

2. Prospect-engaged content

3. Prospect self-attributed traits

4. Prospect demographic information

5. Prospect company information

6. Prospect persona

Prospect-Created Content

Examples of prospect-created content include articles or posts on LinkedIn as well as conference, podcast, or webinar appearances.

Prospecting Becc (see Figure 10.9), we are lucky she is super-active on social media. In particular, she is heavily invested in her must-watch Flip The Script series (available on YouTube).

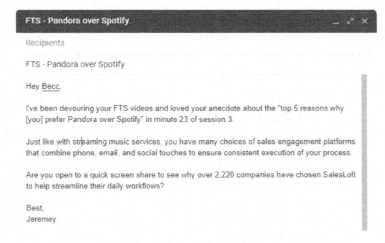

Figure 10.9: Cold email referencing prospect-created content

The most important thing about this email is there is no way a machine could have generated it because of all the little details. A machine would not have known to abbreviate Flip the Script as FTS (we're not even sure Becc does but that's OK). A machine would not have pulled specific and relevant detail from minute 23 of session 3.

The other critical detail is the segue linking the choice of streaming music services to the choice of sales engagement platforms.

In contrast, amateur personalization fails to link the personalized prospect premise to the sellers' solution. For example, Jeremey recently received the email shown in Figure 10.10.

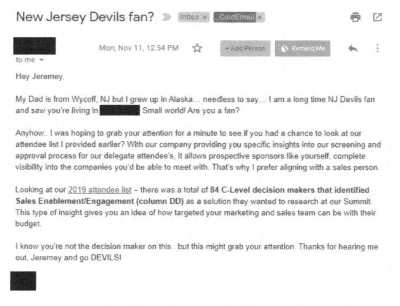

Figure 10.10: Prospecting email lacking context and segue

We are not into rep shaming and we want to give the rep proper respect for his attempt at personalizing. We use this email merely as an example to illustrate what happens when one fails to link personalization to product. Here, there is no link between NJ Devils hockey or Jeremey's hometown and the rep's solution (sponsoring a sales & marketing event). The phrase "Anyhow…" is not segue. Jeremey is not a hockey fan. However, he is hyper-active on LinkedIn so this rep could have targeted him much more effectively.

What would better segue have looked like? How about: "While sponsoring the Devils might be shrewd for Prudential, I'm betting you'll get more bang for your buck targeting sales & marketing professionals at our upcoming summit."

Prospect-Engaged Content

If we could not find prospect-created content for Becc, then we would turn to prospect-engaged content such as comments, shares, or likes on

LinkedIn. These three categories are not created equal. Since comments take the most amount of prospect effort, you should start there.

As it turns out, Becc does like a lot of other content but does not comment often. Precisely because the segue will be a stretch, we choose her comment shown in Figure 10.11 (It also helps that Becc worked at G2 so we are guessing she knows Ryan directly).

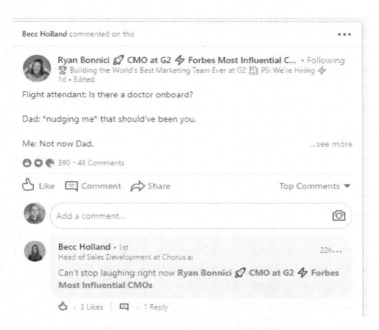

Figure 10.11: Example of prospect-engaged content

Our email to Becc based on her comment is shown in Figure 10.12.

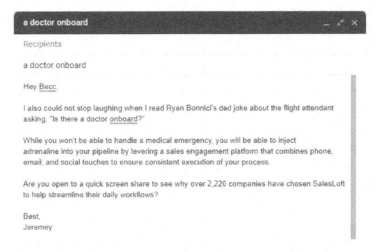

a doctor onboard

Recipients

a doctor onboard

Hey Becc,

I also could not stop laughing when I read Ryan Bonnici's dad joke about the flight attendant asking, "Is there a doctor onboard?"

While you won't be able to handle a medical emergency, you will be able to inject adrenaline into your pipeline by levering a sales engagement platform that combines phone, email, and social touches to ensure consistent execution of your process.

Are you open to a quick screen share to see why over 2,220 companies have chosen SalesLoft to help streamline their daily workflows?

Best,
Jeremey

Figure 10.12: Cold email referencing prospect-engaged content

Prospect Self-Attributed Traits

Self-attributed traits are found in the Headline, About, and Experience sections of your prospect's LinkedIn profile.

Becc's headline (Head of Sales Development at Chorus.ai) and background image do not give us much to work with (see Figure 10.13).

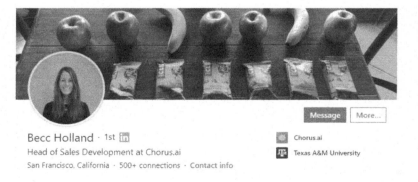

Becc Holland · 1st
Head of Sales Development at Chorus.ai
San Francisco, California · 500+ connections · Contact info

Message   More...

Chorus.ai
Texas A&M University

Figure 10.13: Becc Holland's headline and background image

Similarly, Becc's experience section does not provide any detail (see Figure 10.14).

Experience

Head of Sales Development
Chorus.ai
Jul 2019 – Present · 5 mos
San Francisco Bay Area

Figure 10.14: Becc Holland's recent career experience

Then, we strike pay dirt in her About section as shown in Figure 10.15.

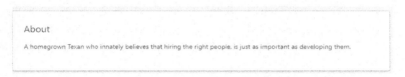

About

A homegrown Texan who innately believes that hiring the right people, is just as important as developing them.

Figure 10.15: Becc Holland's About section on LinkedIn

With something to work with, we craft the prospect self-attributed traits email provided in Figure 10.16.

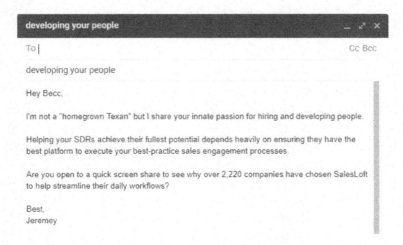

developing your people _ ⤢ ×

To | Cc Bcc

developing your people

Hey Becc,

I'm not a "homegrown Texan" but I share your innate passion for hiring and developing people.

Helping your SDRs achieve their fullest potential depends heavily on ensuring they have the best platform to execute your best-practice sales engagement processes.

Are you open to a quick screen share to see why over 2,220 companies have chosen SalesLoft to help streamline their daily workflows?

Best,
Jeremey

Figure 10.16: Cold email referencing prospect self-attributed traits

Prospect Demographic Information

Hopefully, you will have been able to personalize with prospect-created content, prospect-engaged content, or prospect self-attributed traits.

Personalizing using prospect demographic information the first category falling into the "something is better than nothing" category. As with the prior examples, the key here is to show that a human (you) put in real time and effort.

Demographic information includes career experience, education, volunteer experience, recommendations given or received, accomplishments, hobbies, etc. Much of this can be found to varying extents in LinkedIn or via web search.

Here, you want to look for legitimate commonalities if possible. As it turns out, we have very little in common with Becc. We do have a whopping 1,064 mutual connections but we are not a big fan of referencing that since it is impersonal.

Here, we leverage a recent recommendation Becc received from her former colleague (see Figure 10.17).

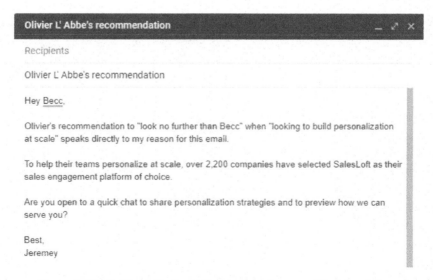

Figure 10.17: Cold email referencing prospect demographic information

Prospect Company Information

For people who have a limited web footprint, your next best hope is to leverage information about their company. This may include press releases, financial disclosures, executive hiring, M&A, blog posts or other content marketing, website copy, etc.

In Figure 10.18, we personalize using a tagline from Becc's company's homepage. We included an image of the website for two reasons. First, SalesLoft data science shows including one highly relevant image boosts the reply rate. Second, there is a good chance your prospect has not been to their company's homepage recently.

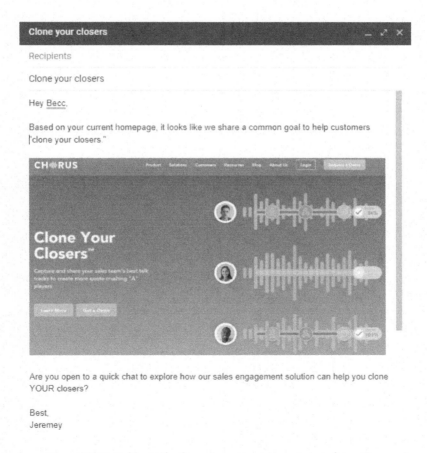

Figure 10.18: Cold email referencing prospect company information

Prospect Persona

Worst case, if you do not have a relevant prospect or prospect company premise, then you can at least personalize on their role as shown in Figure 10.19.

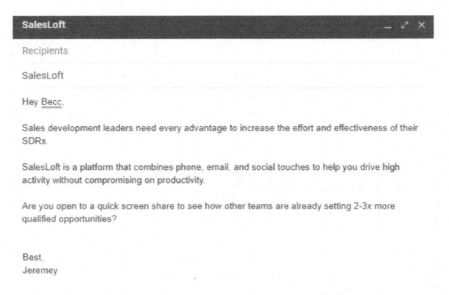

Figure 10.19: Cold email referencing the prospect's persona

There is a bit of a trade-off between the degree of email personalization and the amount of activity any rep can complete. While each organization will need to decide the right mix, all signs seem to be pointing at consistent personalization being table stakes as prospects ignore un-personalized and dynamically personalized (i.e. machine personalized) emails.

Cheat Sheet for Crafting High-Response Emails

- A/B test

- Optimize the entire email – subject, greeting, and body

- Write simply

- Keep emails to <100 words

- Your value prop should clearly state the "what", "how" and "why" of your offering

- At a minimum, emails should be customized by persona and industry

CHAPTER 11
Structuring Cold Calls

Because only one in every sixteen calls[54] leads to a meaningful conversation, it's extremely important that SDRs be highly skilled in converting cold calls into warm leads. In this chapter we aim to provide to framework to help you effectively engage and convert contacts...

Leaving Voicemails

Most SDR calls go unanswered which is why we think it's important to begin this chapter with a discussion of the most effective way to leave voicemails. The first rule we need SDRs to follow is that they should leave a series of three voicemails in any given cadence--once at the beginning, once in the middle, and once at the end.

That being said, SDRs also need to accept the hard truth that they should never expect prospects to call them back. Nonetheless, the purpose of leaving voicemails is to direct a prospect's attention to the emails they will also send just before or after dropping the voicemail. That is why voicemails need to be kept short and sweet, as in the following: "Hi, this is <<SDR full name>> from <<SDR company>>. I'd like to share a couple ideas with you on <<relevant and valuable topic >>. Simply reply to the email I just sent so we can set up time to talk." That is all that needs be said. Through this is a very efficient email script in and of itself, the SDR could also provide their phone number, but we feel that simply wastes time.

Converting Cold Calls into Warm Leads

By adopting an organization-wide sales methodology in which all sales professionals in an organization are trained and coached is the most efficient starting point for ensuring that cold calls turn into warm leads. If you are a sales development leader and your organization does not such a methodology, then adopt one of your choosing to help give your SDRs the best chance of being fearless on the phone. We believe that methodologies are systems that facilitate creativity. By coaching SDRs through this type of strong framework, they will be able to direct their energy toward asking questions, listening, and guiding, rather than just figuring out how to control the conversation. Holistically, any methodology should include pre-call planning, call structure, and post-call follow-up.

The Importance of Pre-Call Planning

Even devoting as little as five or ten minutes to pre-call planning can make a big difference when it comes to call success. This is because putting time into research actually helps SDRs save time by not calling people who aren't a good fit. Next, prospects tend to be far more receptive when SDRs engage them with an understanding of their industry, company, and role. We have listened to too many call recordings where SDRs dance the soft-shoe shuffle when prospects confront them with, "Do you even know what we do?" Such calls rarely if ever convert to opportunities and, even worse, burn a longer-term bridge. Through researching the prospect in advance SDRs can match value messaging to a prospect's most likely use cases. Finally, the mere act of preparing bolsters confidence by imparting knowledge and with it comes a feeling of power and confidence. Confident SDRs are more likely to have product prospect conversations and generate opportunities.

Surprisingly, we don't take much notice at what it means to be confident on the phone, so we tracked down academic research[55] to justify the prior statement linking communication and sales success. Joe Downing of

Pennsylvania State University partnered with a group of experts to compile a 10-item sales communication rating instrument. Mr. Downing then engaged a different set of experts to rate a group of 45 sales agents in a call center. By using conversion data, he separated the agents into quartiles to identify the communication style differences between top-performing and bottom-performing reps.

Communication Strengths of Top Performers

Downing's study found the following strengths exhibited most by top-performers, they:

- Spoke at an appropriate rate

- Emphasized important points with changes in pitch and volume

- Spoke in language that the customer could understand

- Used short, affirmative words and sounds to indicate listening to the customer

- Acknowledged or paraphrased what the customer said

How Top- and Bottom Performers Compare

In order to present a complete picture, we thought it would be a good idea to show all top-performers were not statistically different using Downing's remaining five ratings criteria. All performers, no matter what their level:

- Remained calm and friendly

- Completed his/her thoughts

- Spoke at an appropriate volume

- Talked without vocalizing pauses ("um," "like," "you know," etc.)

- Did not interrupt the customer in mid-sentence

What's at Stake During a Sales Call

Tying pre-call research and this academic study back to sales development, consider that most SDRs are early career professionals. Moreover, these individuals must call senior executives with decades of work experience who work for companies ranging from successful startups to global conglomerates. This is a downright intimidating task. It seems logical to us that a modicum of pre-call research should help SDRs exhibit the five traits of top-performers enumerated above.

To further bolster confidence, we regularly remind SDRs they need not be as expert as the prospects they engage; it is sufficient to possess a basic level of knowledge about the prospect's industry and role. The expertise the SDR must bring to the conversation is about how to link product or service to industry and role specific value. In the abstract, return-on-investment ties to one or more levers such as increased revenue, reduced cost, lower risk/uncertainty, lower effort, higher productivity, or less time. This more concrete example shows how SDRs must reference use cases that matter to the prospect: A corporate catering company calling on the head of human resources might cite higher employee engagement (reduced cost, higher productivity) as a key benefit of providing free or subsidized meals.

SDRs also find it liberating to lower the stakes of their calls if the goal is not necessarily to get a meeting or qualify an opportunity, but rather, to merely understand if the person might be a fit for their product or service and qualify or disqualify, accordingly. In this case, if the prospect turns out to be the right person, great and even when not, the SDR still creates value by preventing a poor prospect from entering the funnel in the first place. Even if the person is disqualified the SDR must next assess if the account might still be qualified. If yes, the SDR should then get guidance on the best person with whom to speak, or, even better, seek a referral.

The Mechanics of a Successful Cold Call

It's now time to dive into the mechanics of a successful cold call. Giving credit where credit is due, the following is heavily derived from guidance we received from David Fischer, a Sandler trainer, but further modified by using our own research and experience.

Phase I: Rapport

When a prospect picks up the phone, SDRs have 10 seconds to build enough rapport to earn the right to another 30 seconds. We recommend starting directly with, "Hi <<prospect first name>>, this is <<SDR first and last name>> from <<SDR company name>>. [Pause]" A friendly greeting like "Hi" or "Hey" starts the call off less formally compared to aggressively diving in with, "Jane, this is…" Unless one is calling on prospects that use formal titles (physicians, for example), the vast majority of business professionals at all levels prefer to be addressed by their first names. However, to add authority in a way that fosters equal business stature, SDRs should state their own full names[56].

A debate rages around whether SDRs need to also state their company name before the prospect responds. We fall into the "be up front" camp. Independent of stating company name, the prospect's first words will usually be something along the lines of, "What can I do for you?," "How can I help you?" or even, "OK." SDRs from other organizations regularly prospect us and we find it gimmicky or even evasive when callers withhold their company name.

Pauses like the one we recommend right after the suggested opening lines, above, are an SDR's best friend. Uncomfortable silence, too, often gets the prospect to open the door with lines such as, "Sorry, who is this?" or "Where are you calling from?" or, best of all, "How can I help you?"

Having also spent time on the receiving end of SDR calls, we know the two emotions people generally experience in the moments after a caller introduces themselves. The first is regret at having picked up the phone, because it interrupts workflow. The second is defensiveness, honed from years of self-training to guard our pocketbook and time. The best SDRs can hope to do in this case is to grab a prospect's attention by using a pattern interrupt. This is just what it sounds like, it is a statement that interrupts with an unexpected turn of phrase that encourage a prospect to pay attention.

In contrast to launching right in with a declarative statement such as "I'll cut right to the chase…", we coach SDRs to ask questions. Though it was once the go-to phrase that worked best, "How are you?" has fallen out of fashion due to its very run-of-the-mill nature. As we write this, "How have you been?" is the opening statement sweeping the sales development world. One study[57], based on 90,380 calls, showed this phrase is correlated with a 6.6x increase in the success rate of booking a meeting. Since pattern interrupts like this do lose efficacy as they become commonplace, each SDR should continually experiment with the pattern interrupts that work for them and that they find authentic. If an SDR is not comfortable with a particular pattern interrupt, then it will not work well for them even if it tests well in general.

Contextually appropriate humor also works well if an SDR is comfortable using it. One SDR on our team calls out the elephant in the room by asking, "Do you already regret picking up the phone?" Many of her prospects find this immediately disarming.

Since so many studies are available online, we urge SDRs to complement their gut instinct with web searches. By way of example, we still hear many SDRs ask, "Did I catch you at a bad time?" The rationale behind this question is as follows. Prospects are in automatic "no" mode early on. Hence, asking the opposite, "Did I catch you at a good time?", demands an apology. Asking the "bad time" version and getting a "no" back theoretically implies the prospect is happy to talk. But, surprisingly, a study[58] by Gong reveals that using "Did I catch you at a bad time?" correlates with a 40% decrease in booking meetings.

In addition, asking questions can give clues to a client's personality profile and benefit in getting them talking early. For instance, Expressive and Amiable personality types are more likely to respond with some detail when asked how they have been with Driver and Analytical personality types tending toward single word responses such as "Good."

Phase II: Up-Front Contract

After briefly establishing rapport, the second phase of the cold call framework is delivering an abbreviated up-front contract[59] including time, your agenda, and suggested next steps. For example: "The reason for my call is [that] I work with a <<prospect role>> professionals like yourself across the <<prospect industry>>. I'll take just two minutes of your time to share what we're doing with them and then you can tell me if it makes sense to continue this conversation at a time that is more convenient for you. Does that sound fair?"

With this statement we set a limited expectation on time, implied value by sharing insights into what competitors are doing, and offer the prospect a degree of control. In addition, we love asking "Does that sound fair?" because asking for just two minutes to preview value is respectful, is a tiny ask, and nearly always elicits the response, "Yeah, that sounds fair or "sure, go ahead.""

With permission to proceed, the SDR transitions into sharing their value proposition; we often refer to this as their "commercial." Here, the goal is to ensure the prospect understands what you do. In a clear, concise, jargon free package, SDRs must share the why, what, and how of their product or service. Take our earlier example of an SDR engaging an HR leader with a daily corporate catering service. "Seamless is a food ordering and delivery service. Our HR clients at New York tech companies tell us the service increases employee engagement by allowing their associates to save time and to eat what they want when they want it. [Pause]"

Notice the first sentence is the "what" and the second sentence provides a person-specific "why" and "how." The "clients tell us" language in the second sentence is important. During cold calls, prospects do not care about you or your company, instead they care about what other people like them are doing right now to add value to their businesses. This is commonly called client voice and should be leveraged frequently and with as much specificity as possible. It is even more powerful if SDRs have permission to cite specific people at specific companies.

The all-telling pause stands in for the cliché "Is that something you might be interested in?" by giving the prospect the opportunity to respond. If SDRs find prospects use this pause to dismiss them, then a question such as the following will help guide the call: "Are you already using a service like us?" or "What initiatives do you have in place to bolster employee engagement?" or, simply, "How does that resonate with you?"

The moment after delivering a commercial is the riskiest part of a cold call since this is where a prospect often responds, "I'm sorry, I'm not interested." Getting past this almost automatic objection requires confidence and skill.

The standard way to navigate through this initial objection is to ask, "I appreciate your sharing that. Would you mind giving me a sense of why you think this might not be a fit for you?" A more creative approach is to ask, "I appreciate your sharing that. Are you saying that increasing employee engagement is not a part of your mandate?" If the response is "no" , then the prospect is not a good fit and the SDR should shift toward getting a referral to the prospect's colleague who is in charge of such decisions.

The CEO of one of our employers was asked about the most impressive cold call he had ever received. After the CEO said he was not interested, the SDR said, "Are you sure you want to do that? [Pause]" This bold move impressed our leader and bought the SDR an extra few minutes to engage.

Phase III: Pain/Discovery
The pain/discovery phase begins when the prospect responds positively to the commercial or, at the very least, when the SDR breaks through early resistance. We want to stress that this phase must neither be a presentation

nor an interrogation but rather a dynamic conversation with both parties asking and answering questions. For reference, the average successful cold call lasts five-to-eight minutes during which a rep talks for an average of 44% of that time[60]. Moreover, reps ask an average of five questions, the best of which are open-ended and prompt prospects to respond for at least 30 seconds. Productive cold calls often start by asking the prospect about their critical goals and initiatives and then probing into what is and is not working for them. All the while the SDR is mentally qualifying or disqualifying the prospect by linking prospect wants and needs to the SDR's company's solutions.

Even though average cold calls last just over two minutes (132 seconds)[61], the successful ones last longer. In this short period of time, SDRs should be expected only to complete the highest level of qualification. In most cases this means (a) verifying that the proposed solution addresses at least one of the prospect's pain points, and (b) gathering information on one or two must-have criteria. As far as the latter, the company OwnBackup provides data backup and recovery services for customers using the Salesforce CRM platform. politely disqualifies a prospect, along with their account, who does not use this CRM (or plans to use it in a reasonable time frame. Any additional information provided by the prospect is gravy.

During the pain/discovery conversation, the SDR should expect to be asked questions. Sometimes these will be in the form of objections, sometimes they are simply questions, and, in both cases, they are an SDR's friend, because both questions and objections signal engagement and reveal what prospects care about most. It is a very bad sign when a prospect does not ask questions. If this is the case, the prospect might be just being polite by letting the SDR get through their spiel. To counter any silence, SDRs need to pause frequently to encourage prospects to fill the uncomfortable silence.

Five Steps for Handling Objections, Questions, and Silence

This seems like the perfect place to digress into a five-step process designed to specifically handle these inevitabilities. (Ignore the false sales prophets who say great salespeople never get objections because they always prevent them.)

Step 1 Remain silent and actively listen rather than try to think of what to say next. Allow long silences to develop so prospects can fully express themselves.

Step 2 Demonstrate that you understand and empathize with their objection. SDRs should respond, in a non-mechanical way, with, "I appreciate your sharing that <<paraphrased objection>>. You are not the first HR leader who has asked about this."

Step 3 Clarify the objection by asking a question in return. We find this to be the hardest part for SDRs because they have been conditioned for their entire lives, especially in school and at home, to give answers when authority figures ask questions. As a bonus, responding to an executive's question with a clarifying question elevates the SDR's business stature since it positions the rep as a potential thought-partner and not "just" another seller.

Step 4 Respond to the objection, but only after the deeper root cause of an objection is uncovered. While we do not have an exact framework, we do suggest to always reply to simple objections with simple answers. Too often, sales professionals respond to questions and objections by stuffing everything but the kitchen sink into answers. In the absence of non-verbal cues, especially over the phone, long-winded answers imply either trickery or complexity from the perspective of the prospect. Even when more nuanced answers are warranted, SDRs should start with "That's easy" or "That's normal" and then dive into "Here's how we do that..." Last, bolster responses with brief value stories whenever possible while illustrating how your other clients solved the very challenge raised by the prospect.

Step 5 Confirm the objection or question has been addressed to the satisfaction of the prospect. Rather than asking "Does that makes sense?", the best SDRs ask open-ended questions such as "What else can I clarify about <<objection>>?" Or, if the SDR has a sense the response might require the prospect to change their thinking or processes, one could ask, "How is this different from what you were expecting?" or "In what way is this different from what you are doing today?" Regardless of which question the SDR asks, they should listen very carefully to the tone of the response to pick up any negative subtext.

Sales teams (SDR leaders and their AE leader partners) must align on how they want frequently asked questions to be answered. Two areas we find are in most need of alignment are pricing, which comes up an average of once or twice on a cold call[62], along with the subject of competition, which comes up once on an average cold call[63]. Since these questions are unavoidable, SDRs must either be coached both on direct answers and how to answer without coming off as evasive.

A direct answer would sound something like, "Our pricing ranges from $120K to $150K. Is that in the ballpark of what you were expecting?" In this case, the lower end of the range should be upper bound for what the prospect will end up paying. Why? Think about when someone quotes you a range. You probably believe only suckers pay anything above the lower bound let alone anything close to the upper bound.

When rules demand SDRs defer pricing conversations it is effective to demonstrate empathy and honesty by saying, "People ask about pricing on pretty much every call. I wish I could give you a range, but I don't want to mislead you one way or the other. Our pricing depends on a variety of different inputs that we can talk through on the next call to provide you with a clear answer. Does that sound fair?"

Phase IV: Closing

Closing SDRs usually means scheduling a follow-up call. However, defining Phase four this way implies there is a clean transition point from the pain/discovery phase, but in the real world a closing requires far more art than science in that it requires SDRs to sense the moment when a qualified prospect feels there is value in continuing the discussion.

Prospects rarely, if ever, come out and say, "Listen, I've got to run in a minute so let's set up time to continue chatting." Instead, we coach SDRs to listen for signs of curiosity. This, again, is why questions or even objections are so valuable. SDRs can push to close even in mid-conversation by leaning on the up-front-contract as follows, "I know I called you out of the blue and I promised to only take two minutes of your time. Given what you said about <<relevant pain point>>, it feels like this might be a fit for you. How does your calendar look on Thursday at 2 p.m. to continue the conversation?"

While many prospects who get to this stage in the conversation will agree to a meeting, some will continue to push back because you are demanding more of their most precious non-renewable resource, time. Here is where staying "behind the pendulum" – another Sandler Training technique – comes into play. Imagine a prospect's willingness to accept a follow up meeting is represented by a pendulum. When the pendulum swings left, their willingness goes down; when the pendulum swings right, their willingness goes up. Staying "behind the pendulum" means that no matter where your prospect is, the rep should always be slightly to the left. Somewhat counter-intuitively, if the prospect resists the push to close, the rep should not aggressively pull the prospect to the right by singing the praises of their product or service. A "behind the pendulum" close for a SaaS product sounds like, "Given the nature of our product, clients tell us it's really something better understood seen vs. described over the phone. Do you have time tomorrow afternoon for us to show you a demonstration of the platform? Within the first 15 minutes, you'll be able to decide whether this is a fit for you. If you decide it is not, we can end the call and part ways. No worries."

We love this approach because it catches people off-guard. Prospects expect salespeople to be aggressive. Staying "behind-the-pendulum" is soft-selling at its best. Rather than pushing the prospect forward, the prospect sets the tone and maintains a degree of control. To be clear, the SDR controls the process, but the prospect maintains control of their own interest and perception of value.

To minimize no-show rates, a topic we will expand further upon below, SDRs need to do the following while the prospect is still on the call.

Get the prospect to accept the meeting invite right then and there. Simply say: "I just sent over a calendar invite for Thursday at 2 p.m. like we agreed. With firewalls what they are these days, I just want to make sure my email went through. Can confirm you received it by accepting the invite?"

Get the prospect's cell phone number. "Can you please share your cell phone number? I won't put it in our system; I'll just add it to the invite along with mine. That way, I can text you a confirmation just before the call and you can reach me if you are running late."

Phase V: Meeting Contract

Once an SDR sets up a date and time for the next meeting, their work is not quite done. The last thing they need to do is to set expectations for the next meeting using the familiar up-front contract format:

- Time: "To confirm, we scheduled a 30-minute call for next Thursday at 2 p."

- Sales Agenda: "During that call, we will cover <<your agenda>>. To make the best use of your time, can you please share any key projects to which you think our solution might be relevant and we can use to customize that call and make it a good use of your time?" ... "Great, I'll bring <<AE name>> on our side up to speed so she can share relevant examples."

- Prospect Agenda: "In addition, what else would you like to cover?"

- Next step: "Again, the call will be another opportunity to assess whether or not we are able to help you. If at any point during that call you don't feel there is a fit, just let us know."

When describing the Sales Agenda we implore SDRs to be as honest as possible. In many B2B sales the first scheduled meeting is a deeper discovery call. As buyers ourselves we know we have to jump through this hoop, but we do not like doing it. We want to see a demo and we want to get some value out of the call. If you do not demo on that call, then be clear about not doing that as well as clear about what value we will get by being on the call. Importantly, buyers merely learning about a product does not constitute value since they can save time and energy by browsing a website.

Minimizing No-Show Rates

The moment the SDR hangs up it is assumed that the prospect stops thinking about the also company or its solutions. Worse, any garnered interest has probably also melted away to the extent that the prospect will either cancel the call at the last minute or simply ghost the meeting. For context, no-show rates above 20% are bad, 10% to 20% are average, and below 10% are good. Note: These are rates we have observed for disqualifying SDR-sourced leads and not necessarily single meeting no-show rates since SDRs must follow up on no-shows. TOPO's 2019 Sales Development Benchmark report supports these statistics. The report reveals 41% of SDR-qualified leads do not become sales opportunities. Of the 41%, about half are a result of no-shows. Thus, the no-show benchmark is 20%.

18 BEST PRACTICES FOR MINIMIZING
NO-SHOW RATES (prioritized by impact)

1. Book meetings only with prospects pre-qualified (persona & ICP) to buy from you in the first place. (Yes, this one is obvious but critical.)

2. Schedule calls to be held as soon as possible, preferably within five business days and certainly no more than ten business days out.

3. When scheduling the meeting, get the prospect's cell phone number. Text them a personalized meeting reminder the morning of the meeting. (If they run late, you'll also be able to text or call them directly.)

4. If the meeting is booked during a cold call, have the prospect accept the invite while they are still on the call.

5. If the SDR attempted to arrange the meeting via email, then resend the invite if the prospect has not accepted it within 48 hours. Send a thank you when they accept.

6. Send a reminder (email or text) a few hours before the scheduled meeting time. For morning meetings, send the reminder at the end of your prior workday. Sending the confirmation too far in advance, say 24-hours, can increase cancellations since it gives prospects too much opportunity to have second thoughts. (Optionally, call to confirm if you and/or the prospect are bringing considerable resources to bear on the meeting, for example, multiple senior executives, travel, etc.)

7. If your meeting is scheduled more than two weeks out (per #2 avoid this whenever possible), send them valuable content at least once per week to keep them engaged.

8. Call the prospect rather than having them dial into a conference bridge

9. Avoid weak language in the reminder, such as, "Does this time still work for you?" Instead, presume that the meeting will happen. For example, "We are excited to show you a demo tomorrow at ___. We will give you a call at phone number ____. Talk soon."

10. Sell the value to the prospect of investing their time in the meeting, not the more abstract value of your product. For example, use: "My colleague ___ will be with us and is an expert in companies going through similar challenges as you."

11. Ask a question in your confirmation email. For example, "So I can better prepare, what are you looking to get from our meeting?" or, less formally, "Prepping for our meeting… anything specific you'd like to cover?" While I prefer those open-ended questions, you could ask two or three short-answer diagnostic questions instead.

12. Include a succinct, prospect-centric agenda in your calendar invite. For example, "As promised, we'll use this time to: (a) Learn more about your role and priorities to customize the conversation, (b) share how [persona] professionals in [industry] find value in our partnership, (c) customized demo of our platform, (d) Next steps (If your sales process has a prescribed next step, then state it up-front.)

13. Mention any executives/others on your side that are joining the call to not only preview value but also "raise the stakes" of cancellation.

14. Give your calendar invite a strong, direct, prospect-centric title, not "Follow up" or "Check-in."

15. Email the prospect if they are five minutes late to the call and call them directly if they are ten minutes late.

16. Institute a protocol/process for rescheduling "ghosted" meetings. In my experience, you will be able to reschedule half the no-shows, reducing your overall no-show rate to 10% or better.

17. Where relevant/possible, set onsite rather than phone appointments.

18. Avoid scheduling calls during high no-show rate times. The highest no-show meeting rates occur between 8 a.m. and 10 a.m. and the lowest between 3 p.m. and 5 p.m. No-show rates are somewhat higher on Fridays. (Other than 8 a.m., the absolute variation in no-show rates is quite small.)

Ensuring Professional Handoffs

In addition to minimizing no-show rates, SDRs have a duty to hand off meetings in a way that sets up their AE for success. The most basic element for the SDR in setting this up is by entering detailed notes in their CRM system as soon as possible while the information is fresh. Sales development leaders should help by defining the structure for what data must be entered. Tactically, SDR notes can be implemented in the opportunity object as outlines in one large open-text field or in a set of individual fields. At a minimum, notes should include any required qualification information as well as commentary on any prior opportunities in this account or with this prospect in a different account. Should the CRM not automatically notify the AE, the SDR should also email the AE a copy of the notes.

These notes, along with pre-meeting preparation, are critical to delivering a professional buying experience. Prospects should never have to answer the same questions twice. The best AEs (and SDRs if they participate in the next meeting) start scheduled meetings by recapping and confirming what they learned from the prospect's prior conversation with the SDR. Smooth, professional handoffs provide more time for AEs to build value and trust with prospects during the crucial early points in the relationship.

CHAPTER 12
Measuring and Optimizing Performance

Thisbook is mostly about "micro," or bottom-up, in the sense that we show how to hire, train, and enable individuals to succeed as SDRs and to prepare them to thrive as future account executives; however, this chapter switches to the "macro," or top-down, view since sales development leaders get paid for hitting aggregate business targets.

How many SDRs are needed to hit an overall business target?

By way of example, imagine a company has a $50 million target for new annual recurring revenue (ARR) and a $50,000 average contract value (ACV) per deal. Further, assume the outbound sales development team is responsible contributing 40% of this target, or $20 million. (The other 60% is self-sourced by account executives or by Inbound Marketing). How many SDR hires are needed to hit this target?

To complete this calculation, we need to start out by figuring out how many opportunities SDRs need to source, based on the win rate for deals sourced by SDRs. Here we use the industry benchmark[64] win rate is 20% for deals in the $25K to $75K ACV range. Sales development leaders should be very careful to use the win rate of deals sourced by SDRs rather than the aggregate win rate. Typically, the outbound SDR win rate is lower than the AE self-sourced win rate and always lower than the inbound win rate.

The first time we noticed the win rate for outbound SDR-sourced opportunities was different than the AE self-sourced win rate, we were a bit puzzled. Though we never figured out exactly why this is, we have a very strong hypothesis and it is not one sales leadership likes to hear. Our best guess is that AEs accept some less-than-qualified SDR-sourced opportunities into their pipeline to keep their SDRs happy; SDRs often get paid for qualified opportunities yet AEs face little-or-no repercussion for closing out early stage opportunities. You could engineer for this by tracking the percentage of opportunities closed out suspiciously quickly and add some sort of carrot or stick for AEs to keep the rate down, but that feels to us like a waste of time. Instead, accept the phenomenon as a minor but acceptable gaming of the system. If SDR ROI is strong, we just let it go.

Since ARR = (# opportunities) x (SDR-sourced deal win rate) x (ACV), SDRs must source 2,000 total opportunities per year. Sales development leaders should also know the target SDR-sourced pipeline, though we do not need the number for further calculations, equals $100 million (the SDR-sourced ARR divided by the outbound SDR win rate).

Continuing to work backwards, benchmarks from both TOPO and The Bridge Group reveal 60% of SDR-sourced meetings convert into opportunities. The average no-show rate is around 15% and another 30% of leads are disqualified on other criteria; the math here is (1 - 0.15) x (1 - 0.3) = 0.6. So, creating 2,000 opportunities requires scheduling 2000 / 0.6 = 3,333 meetings.

The next metric we need to know concerns how many activities—phone calls, emails, social touches, and research steps—it takes to schedule a meeting. To figure this out, we need two more benchmarks. The first is 20 meetings scheduled per SDR per month[65] and the second is 2000 activities per SDR per month. By using these two numbers we calculate that it takes

100 activities to schedule one meeting. Hence, our 3,333 meetings will take whopping 333,333 activities.

Don't be fooled into thinking we now we have all the information we need to calculate the number of SDRs required to achieve the $20 million business target. The naïve calculation is 333,333 activities divided by 24,000 activities per SDR per year which yields just shy of 14 SDRs. But SDR leaders will miss target if they stop here because it assumes zero turnover and that all SDRs are fully ramped for the entire year.

The benchmark for combined voluntary and involuntary attrition, inclusive of promotion to account executive, is 40%. We could create a very complex model by going through many of the above metrics for ramping SDRs, however, there is a simpler way that provides more-or-less the same answer. Let's assume ramping SDRs are half as productive as tenured SDRs due to a combination of lower activity and effectiveness. Therefore, if 40% of SDRs are half as productive, you need an extra 14 x 40% = 6 reps to hit quota. So the total number of SDRs needed to achieve quota is 20.

Bonus calculation - SDR ROI: In Chapter 6, Compensating Talent, we pointed out that SDR compensation varies between $65K and $, depending on region. If we use the midpoint of $75K and add 20% for "fringe" costs[66] and another $5,000 per year for tools[67], this gets us to $95K per SDR or $1.9M for the 20-person team. By contributing $20 million, the sales development team in this example provides a strong 10x ROI.

Your Mileage will Vary

SDR benchmarks published by syndicated research firms like TOPO and The Bridge Group are collected via survey rather than looking at actual CRM data. We believe sales development leaders provide numbers for their tenured SDRs. Since capacity and productivity fluctuate with attrition, one should not be surprised if their numbers are not a rosy as the benchmarks.

In addition to attrition, companies tend to have wide variation in several key assumptions. Table 12.1 shows what happens to ROI as two metrics, the win rate for SDR-sourced opportunities and the number of activities per meeting scheduled, vary.

Win Rate →	10%	15%	20%
100 activities	5.3x	7.8x	10.5x
150 activities	3.6x	5.3x	7.0x
200 activities	2.7x	4.0x	5.3x

Table 12.1 ROI as a function of win rate and activities per meeting scheduled

Building a Sales Development Dashboard

We can construct a dashboard for sales development leaders by extracting the metrics from the example above. We start by grouping them into our three favorite categories: results, effectiveness, and activities. Sales development leaders (Directors and Vice Presidents) should track these in aggregate; first-line sales development managers should stack rank their SDRs on the following metrics.)

- Results
    - SDR ROI (or its reciprocal, SDR cost of sale)
    - SDR-sourced ARR
    - SDR-sourced pipeline
    - ACV of SDR -sourced wins
    - Win rate for SDR-sourced opportunities
    - Average qualified opportunities per SDR per month (benchmark = 10 to 12)
- Effectiveness
    - No-show rate (benchmark = 15%)
    - Disqualification rate after initial meetings held (benchmark = 30%)
    - Activities per qualified opportunity generated
    - Total attrition (benchmark = 40%)

- Activities (and Inputs)

  o Activities per SDR per month (benchmark = 2,000)

  o SDR headcount

  o Percentage of first emails personalized (target = 100%)

  o SLA compliance metrics

  o Average contacts engaged per account per month

  o Average accounts engaged per SDR per month

As an astute reader you will notice we modified a few metrics and added others.

Rather than tracking the average number of meetings scheduled per SDR per month, we suggest sales development leaders focus on average opportunities per SDR per month (or both) for two reasons. First, this is the most common compensation metric. Second, is that you can derive the meetings number from the opportunities number using the no-show and disqualification rate metrics. By following this same logic, we recommend monitoring activities per opportunity generated rather than per meeting scheduled.

We also added four activity metrics. Because the practice doubles reply rates, we track the percentage of first emails personalized--the percentage of emails with any personalization, not the % of each email personalized--which should be around 20%. Admittedly, this can be complex to measure, so in addition, we added a category for SLA compliance metrics. For instance, many SDR:AE service-level-agreements require the primary contact on an opportunity to hold a title of Director or higher; this is hard to police and will drift if not inspected. Finally, we added metrics for contact- and account-engagement to assess the depth and breadth of prospecting.

Track and Optimize

To avoid repeating what we have already covered in previous chapters, we will concentrate only on strategic guidance on optimization in this chapter. Importantly, the results metrics are outputs of activity and effectiveness. While sales development leaders should report on them, managers can only control activity and effectiveness via motivation and coaching.

Both the activity and effectiveness metrics are important; however, leaders must prioritize levers with the highest return-on-effort at any given time. The levers, in turn, have sub-levers. For example, if no-show rates are too high, sales development leaders can turn to the 18 techniques we shared in Chapter 11.

Activity per SDR per month is the one metric to rule them all. To drive this metric we stress the importance of managers holding every SDR accountable to delivering a minimum number of calls each day. Every rep, every day. If an organization expects SDRs to make 300 calls per week, then managers must hold SDRs accountable to 60 calls each day. When managers fail to do this, SDRs fall behind. Once managers finally do notice, typically on a Thursday afternoon, SDRs will not have enough time to recover. Notice that we focus on calls rather than total activities for the simple reason that calls are not only the hardest activity but they also act as the canary in the coal mine. Nearly all SDRs execute their workflow using sales engagement software. Since calls are part of multi-touch cadences, when the calls happen then the emails and social touches follow automatically. Moreover, when calls happen, then new contacts are almost certainly added to cadences.

It is not uncommon for new SDR managers to challenge us on the daily call rule, especially those who were successful in organizations that lack this level of inspection. Our counter is that people who make it to SDR managers are top SDRs, not average ones. Average SDRs need guidance to stay on track and holding SDRs accountable in this way is actually an act of compassion because those who meet activity goals succeed and those who do not fail.

The other suggestion we often hear from new managers is to only hold SDRs to daily call targets if they have not scheduled a meeting. They fear the focus on activity will come at the expense of effectiveness. In truth, we care about both. If an SDR is able to book a meeting on their 30th call, then they should keep going and book another one by their 60th. SDRs and their managers should have every incentive to do this because they will make more money, feel less stress by virtue of hitting quota sooner, and get promoted faster.

The biggest career mistakes are not strategy errors, but rather are rather the challenges we create when we take our eyes off one or more of the activity and effectiveness metrics. To be sure, successful sales development leaders are the ones who establish targets for every one of these metrics, track them religiously, and optimize them relentlessly.

CHAPTER 13

Structuring Sales Development

After years of building and running our fair share of sales development teams at startups and large companies we have iterated our way into a set of strongly held best-practices. What you will learn in this chapter is intended to save you the pain of making the same mistakes we did. To that end, and in order to make it as easy as possible for you to put this knowledge to work, we have structured our advice in easy to follow tips. We are also aware that everyone's experiences are not exactly the same, therefore our tips come with "exceptions", which we will also note.

Tip : Insource Sales Development
We assume you have already decided that the sales development function makes sense for your go-to-market motion or you already have a sales development team you want to optimize. That means you have product-market fit, your customer acquisition cost supports having the function, and you do not have an extremely fast, transactional sale. Given this starting point, the main decision sales leadership must wrestle with is whether to insource or to outsource.

In regard to outsourcing, if there is anything to learn from our experience, know that we have worked with leading sales development outsourcing providers and have failed every time. Moreover, we've also asked everyone we know and have heard the same thing. In fact, we've yet to hear of any truly successful outsourcing projects. That doesn't mean that we haven't experienced or heard of others experiencing mild successes. These are usually found in instances where sales and marketing leaders were executing a very lightweight motion, such as driving event attendance or following up on inbound leads.

Based on what we've heard and experienced, the causes of outsourced sales development failures are rooted in communication issues and talent issues.

On the communication side, most outsourced sales development partners have an engagement manager with whom meetings are set roughly once-per-week. In addition, this engagement manager seldom manages directly the actual SDRs supporting you. Unless your sales development processes are already fully tuned (which is never the case) and the engagement manager and outsourced SDR manager fully understand your processes (also never the case), this setup is designed to fail. Our experience has taught us that in order for sales development to work in an organization SDRs, managers, AEs, marketing, and all other internal business partners must engage in constant dialogue.

On the talent side, remember that the individuals working for sales development outsourcing shops are not of the same caliber as you would select when using the rigorous hiring practices we recommend in this book. Though a sweeping generalization, we've taken notice of a substantially high turnover rate among SDRs working for outsourcers. Just think of what you endure when just one of your assigned resources leaves and you must start the time-consuming, non-trivial exercise of training a new one.

Let's suspend disbelief for a moment and assume an outsourcer has such flawless communication and talent that they are capable of delivering high quality opportunities at the expected rate. Even with that, the significant problem, specifically that SDRs are your best AE talent pipeline, remains. Let's illustrate by exploring the economic impact of promoting from within using simple math and the following assumptions:

- AE OTE is $120K with $60K base salary and $60K variable compensation target

- AE quota is $600K

- Commissions are paid linearly from "dollar one" at a rate of 10%.

- AE tenure is 2 years

- On average, 80% of SDRs promoted from within to AEs are successful compared to 50% of experienced AEs hired from the outside. Success means hitting quota. Failure means hitting 50% of quota.

Given the numbers above, a successful AE, whether hired from inside or outside, generates $1.2 million and costs $240K over two years--yielding profit of $960. An unsuccessful AE generates $600K and costs $180K–yielding profit of $420K. Consider that 80% of SDRs hired from the inside are successful, the expected profit for an AE promoted internally from SDR is (80% x $960K) + (20% x $420K) = $852K. Whereas 50% of AEs brought in from the outside are successful, the expected profit for external hires is (50% x $960K) + (50% x $420K) = $690K.

Whether or not you opted to follow the above math know that the bottom line shows that promoting from within versus hiring from outside yields an extra $162K in profit ($852K - $690K). To give you even more incentive to hire from within, know that this amount is enough to cover the two-year salary cost of most SDRs! And I am sure you can already hear us saying that SDR programs pay for themselves based solely on the impact of training people to be AEs. Any additional profit SDRs generate from sourcing opportunities is gravy.

The only exception we can think of that justifies outsourcing sales development is when SDRs engage only inbound leads and there is no

SDR-to-AE promotion path. We have seen the latter condition benefit companies that sell very large ($250K or higher) deals and, therefore, require highly experienced salespeople.

Some of you may argue that it is better to outsource the SDR function when there is not enough scale to hire an SDR manager. We counter that with the fact that this is the most dangerous time to outsource the function based on the communication and talent issues discussed above. When you are setting up a new sales development function you need constant and open communication along with the best possible talent if you want to build out repeatable process (inclusive of cadences, messaging, activity expectations, etc.) and robust technology stacks.

Tip 2: Have SDRs Report to (Dedicated SDR) Managers

Leaders often entertain the notion of having SDRs report directly to the AEs they support--especially when they deal with a small number of SDRs. This is a terrible idea no matter how you look at it. Remember that an AE's job is to sell, not to manage. Consequently, an AE does not have the time, motivation, or expertise to coach SDRs and to hold SDRs accountable to required activities. The worst we have seen is when AEs treat "their" SDRs as personal assistants, some going so far as to have them order lunch and pick up dry cleaning.

In taking all of the above information into account, we recommend doing the following:

Start your SDR function by hiring a dedicated
SDR manager and a full team.

If that is too expensive then hire at least two SDRs who will temporarily report to one of three roles until you have enough scale to have a dedicated SDR manager.

The best short-term alternative is to have your SDRs report to your head of sales enablement because that person is built to systematize and to coach.

The next best alternative is to have your SDRs report to the head of sales operations, assuming the person in that position has the experience and leadership chops to handle the job. (Don't even consider this option if your head of sales operations is more focused operationally on metrics and tools.)

The least viable option is to have SDRs report to a first line sales manager who also manages the AEs that the SDRs support. We ranked this option last because a sales manager always gravitates toward AEs who have deals that need support to close; consequently, the SDRs are often ignored and usually fail.

Tip 3: SDR Managers should never be player-coaches

A recruiter friend recently asked us, "Do you know someone who can lead the pace as an individual contributor and can provide player/coach support early on. We replied, "No. And, you should tell your client that is a really bad idea!" (Proving that truth is stranger than fiction, consider that this recruiter also wanted a BDR with at least 5 years of experience in fintech.)

Know that there are great sales managers and there are also great AEs. Similarly, there are great SDRs and there are great SDR managers. However, experience has taught us that people put into player/coach roles are, at best, mediocre at both functions. As per Tip 3, if you cannot hire the number of SDRs to justify a standalone manger, then choose a temporary manager until you build enough scale.

Tip 4: Promote SDR Managers from Within

We once had a policy of recruiting our SDR managers by alternating between internal promotions and external hires. Our rationale for bringing people in from the outside was that they would bring fresh ideas to the function. Sadly, that approach didn't deliver many fresh ideas and we are now totally committed to promoting only from within (assuming we have the interest and talent).

SDRs who are promoted from within have every advantage, including knowing your company and its people, your sales process, your customer personas and industries, your product, messaging, and on top of all that, they know the challenges new SDRs need to overcome. Experience has taught us that it is much more efficient to teach a person the skills they need to be successful SDR manager than it is to attempt to impart all of the aforementioned knowledge.

Promoting from within also gives you the advantage of selecting a coachable person. A coachable person is transparent, vulnerable, and hungry to learn. When we are seeking to promote from within it means we are always on the lookout for the better-than-average performers who are organically sought-out by their peers for advice. To help you promote the best talent, also consider adding a team-captain role to test manager candidates.

Circling back to our initial idea of having new SDRs inject fresh ideas, we do expect all of our SDR managers to be students of the craft through reading constantly and building relationships with peers at other companies. Moreover, we are quite open to hiring the Director/Vice President of Sales Development from outside since they get tactical air-cover from the existing managers but bring strategic wisdom and experience.

Tip 5: Have SDRs Report to Sales

According to benchmark data, 65% of SDRs report into Sales, 24% into Marketing and 11% into other functions[68]. We feel strongly that SDRs should report into Sales regardless of focus--inbound, outbound, or blended--for two reasons;

First, SDRs are the best AE talent pipeline, as we have discussed exhaustively. Most people who take sales development roles want to be AEs, at least when they start, so it behooves you to make the path as clear as possible to attract the best candidates.

Second, having SDRs report into Sales ensures strong target account and contact alignment.

Going one level deeper in the benchmarks, 90% of pure outbound teams report to Sales, 61% of blended teams report to Sales, and 53% of pure inbound teams report to sales. We suspect a large proportion of blended and inbound teams report to Marketing since CMOs want to guarantee follow-up on leads. However, we fear large numbers of marketing qualified leads (MQLs) will be ignored by AEs if sales leadership is not fully accountable. Having blended and inbound teams report to Sales maintains pressure for Sales and Marketing to align, ensures less "junk" is injected at the top of the funnel, and guarantees stronger engagement with qualified leads.

The obvious exception to this rule is if you have a Marketing leader who is exceptionally skilled at running sales development teams and that skill set is missing within your sales organization. In that case, by all means, have SDRs report into Marketing.

Tip 6: Pair SDRs with AEs for Outbound Enterprise and Larger Mid-Market Selling

After a few false starts, we finally arrived at an effective system for structuring SDR teams. Specifically, pairing SDRs 1:1 with AEs for enterprise and larger mid-market selling, albeit with some precise rules around execution. For these types of accounts, patience, persistence, and knowledge are all critical. Also it's best to remember that large accounts usually include more people to engage than one person is able to handle alone.

Pairing is matching SDRs with AEs such that they 'own' the same accounts. Tactically, this translates into having both a sales owner and SDR owner for every account in a CRM. The term pairing usually refers to a 1:1 ratio, however, using the term "pod" simply refers to any N:M combination (1:1, 1:2 ,2:2, etc.) where, again, SDRs and AEs co-own accounts.

Round-Robin and The Pairing Alternative

Round-robin is the alternative to pairing. With round-robin, each opportunity sourced by an SDR gets routed to the next eligible AE and once every AE gets an opportunity the queue restarts. Notably, round-robin appears to have manifold advantages over pairing, including:

- High resilience to AE and SDR headcount variation

- High resilience to AE and SDR quality variation

- Equitable opportunity distribution

- Accurate SDR performance assessment (by removing AE variation as a factor)

- Accurate AE performance assessment

Given the many advantages of the round-robin structure, there are still reasons we would continue to recommend 1:1 AE pairing:

- Opportunity quality. With round-robin, there is limited communication between AEs and SDRs. Hence, SDRs have an ever-present incentive to lob opportunities over the fence. Moreover, since AEs don't know the SDRs that well, they have limited incentive to tell SDRs why any given opportunity is unqualified.

- SDR mentorship. Most often, SDR managers were promoted SDRs. As such, SDR managers do not have experience as AEs. SDR managers are extremely valuable for coaching SDRs to be great at their current job, but AE mentorship is key to developing SDRs to be successful when they get promoted.

We assume you remember that we recommended 1:1 pairing of SDRs with AEs. This is because that with each incremental AE an SDR supports, opportunity quality and both the AE and SDRs incentive to coach each other both diminish. In addition, the whole point of having SDRs is to offload some or all of an AEs prospecting responsibility. The only time we would advocate having an SDR support multiple AEs is when an AE would only need part of an SDR to fill their pipeline. A more likely scenario is when an AE would need a dedicated SDR (or more than one SDR) fill the top of their funnel.

One of the main concerns with 1:1 pairing is the perceived lack of resilience in the event an SDR or an AE leaves or changes role. To deal with this problem, we once built 2:2 pods as shown in Figure 13.1. In this configuration, AE1 partners with SDR1 on 50% of accounts and with SDR2 on the other 50% of accounts; AE2 splits their account in a similar way.

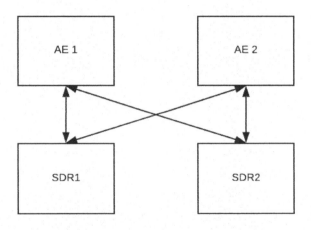

Figure 13.1: 2:2 SDR:AE Pod

In practice, we found 2:2 inferior to 1:1 due to management complexity. Unfortunately, the number of AEs and SDRs is rarely in balance due to SDR turnover (and to a lesser extent to AE turnover). In terms of SDR:AE ratios, we must contend with many instances of 1:2 and 3:2, with other ratios appearing from time to time. In addition, it is important that managers remain hyper-vigilant to ensure equal distribution of opportunities. To elaborate, we've seen instances where, say, AE1 "bonds" with SDR1 such that SDR1 underserves AE2. This is when the precise execution rules we mentioned earlier come into play.

For starters, we do not recommend automatically pairing SDRs with newly hired AEs. New AEs must earn the right to SDR coverage by meeting ramp goals. Depending on the organization and its sales cycles, ramp goals may include activities, the number of qualified opportunities, pipeline, or closed-won business. (The first two metrics must be vetted by sales managers since they are otherwise easily manipulated). For example, we might only assign an SDR in month three to an AE if she has sourced four qualified opportunities during month two.

Next, AEs must earn the right to ongoing SDR coverage. As with ramping AEs, tenured AEs must continue to achieve defined key metrics for activity, opportunity quantity, new pipeline value generated, or closed-won business. Should an AE fail to achieve such metrics for two months, we recommend removing SDR coverage. Though rare, we will also take SDR coverage away from an AE who does not respect our codified SDR:AE rules-of-engagement. To earn SDR coverage back, an AE must achieve target metrics for one (or two) months.

If you are worried about what happens to SDRs as coverage is granted or taken away, it's not that traumatic. When an SDR is removed, the AE is not cut off cold turkey. Rather, the SDR will complete any in-flight cadences. If the SDR is reassigned to another AE, then the SDR engages new contacts on their new partner's accounts. If all AEs are paired, then the SDR is kept at 100% utilization by working 'unassigned' accounts and any meetings they book are distributed in round-robin fashion to any eligible AE.

Perhaps surprisingly, we also reset AE:SDR pairings roughly each quarter. Sales is a meritocracy, not a democracy. Hence, our best SDRs are assigned to our best AEs. We rank SDRs based on qualified meetings held, independent of other compensation plan elements, when stack-ranking for pairings as it removes any pipeline or opportunity variance that could arise as a result of their AE partner. For AEs, we stack rank on percentage of quota attained for the quarter. Don't get the idea that this always means tenured SDRs get matched with tenured AEs because that is only the case about half the time. We find SDRs take great pride in being paired with top AEs and vice-versa. This arrangement has a powerful impact on performance independent of tenure.

Also, don't worry that reshuffling–either monthly due to AEs hitting/missing goals or quarterly due to periodic rebalancing negatively impacts performance. Much to our original surprise, the opposite happens. As previously mentioned, we smooth the impact by having SDRs complete any inflight cadences. More importantly though, we find a performance boosted with this fresh set of eyes. It's not uncommon for SDRs working an account for the first time to find high-quality contacts the prior SDR missed simply because they implemented different techniques or are better motivated.

As for rules-of-engagement, we like to give SDR and AEs a decent amount of leeway as to how they engage accounts. We support AEs and SDRs splitting accounts, dividing accounts by business unit, or dividing up specific contacts. But the one thing we don't condone or recommend is having AEs hunt senior contacts (ex: Directors, VPs, and CxOs) and leaving junior contacts (individual contributors and mangers) to SDRs. One might as well not have SDRs if following this approach.

While we do not recommend pairing one SDR with multiple AEs, we acknowledge that some organizations do choose this structure. The biggest danger is that the SDR will favor one AE over the others. To combat this the SDR manager must ensure disciplined adherence to hunting blocks. For instance, consider an SDR with four hunting blocks (9a-1030a, 11am-1230p, 2p-330p, and 4p-530p) who supports 2 AEs. The SDR must dedicate two of the four hunting blocks each day to AE1 and two to AE2. Equal activity should, over time, deliver equal output.

Tip 7: Use Round-Robin meeting distribution for Smaller Mid-Market and SMB

We are a bit conflicted about recommending round-robin meeting distribution in situations where account coordination is not required. After all, when following the pairing best practices described above, you' would still have each SDR source exclusively for one AE.

We acknowledge our pairing approach requires substantial discipline and that such a high level of care is always warranted when account coordination is critical. In the event an organization or a go-to-market segment is focused on smaller accounts where only one person is needed to engage a more limited set of contacts, we feel round-robin is suitable.

Many companies start with an "open territory" model where AEs and SDRs can claim any account regardless of geography, size, or vertical. When this is the case sales operations often imposes two constraints. First, individuals are subject to an account limit, typically around 40 for Enterprise accounts and 100 to 200 for SMB and mid-market accounts. Second, accounts are up for grabs if the owner has not engaged the account within a set window, often 30 days, but occasionally up to 90 days.

When an organization has relatively few sales professionals and a large number of viable accounts, the open territory model is effective. However, as a sales team grows to the point where the ocean is no longer teeming with relatively easy to catch fish, bad things start to happen. You know there is a problem when AEs and SDRs wait up until midnight to claim good accounts that have just become eligible due to inactivity. In addition, salespeople start spending massive amounts of time combing through the same accounts in their CRM system. Perhaps worst of all, tenured AEs camp out on the best accounts thereby leaving slim pickings for new hires who are then destined to fail.

Given these challenges, we recommend assigning territories to SDRs. We use "territory" broadly to describe traditional territories (combinations of industry, size, and/or geography) or assigned account territories. The optimal approach depends on context.

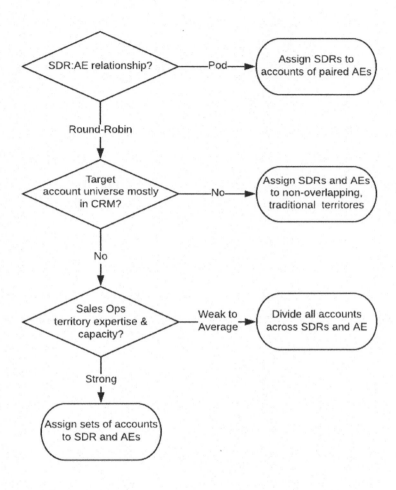

Figure 13.2: Decision tree for SDR (and AE) territory strategy

When AEs are in pods with SDRs, territory assignment for SDRs is trivial–each account has an AE owner and an SDR owner. As mentioned previously, in any structure where an SDR supports multiple AEs, managers must vigilantly monitor activity to ensure SDRs are not playing favorites. If SDRs are paid on opportunity generation, they will gravitate to AEs who are looser with qualification, but if SDRs are paid on a percentage of closed-won bookings, they will gravitate to rainmaking AEs.

When SDRs serve AEs via the round-robin operating model, the next decision to consider is whether the target account universe is mostly in CRM. When selling to SMB, an organization might have millions of target accounts, in which case each SDR (and each AE, assuming AEs are responsible for sourcing some of their own opportunities) is assigned to a non-overlapping territory. We most commonly see this approach implemented with geographic boundaries–states/provinces, postal codes, etc.

If the target account universe is mostly identified in an organization's CRM system then the next consideration is the sophistication of the sales operations team. Most small-to-midsized organizations have weak to moderate territory management expertise and capacity. As a general guideline, if an organization has one (or even no) people fully dedicated to territory management, it then falls into the weak-to-moderate bucket.

Organizations with limited territory management sophistication should divide all accounts across SDRs and AEs. Let's imagine an organization with 60,000 targets accounts in their CRM, 60 AEs, and 60 SDRs. Let's also assume AEs are expected to spend 25% of their time self-sourcing opportunities. Let x equal the number of accounts assigned to each AE. Since SDRs spend 100% of their time sourcing, they need 4x accounts. So, we have (60 AEs * x) + (60 SDRs * 4x) = 300x = 60,000. Hence, x = 200 which means each AE should be assigned 200 accounts and each SDR should be assigned 800 accounts.

If it's just dawned on you that 800 accounts is a lot for a typical SDR to handle, you are probably wondering, there are so many. We worked this example on the basis of the organization's territory management capacity and/or expertise being limited. By assigning territories in this manner there are the added benefits of every account having an engagement owner and that people are not wasting monumental amounts of time identifying and grabbing accounts.

Of course the major disadvantage to assigning 800 accounts at once (and especially 1,000 or 2,000) is that it puts a large "scrubbing" burden on an SDR who (a) should be spending most of their time engaging prospects via phone, email, and social networks, and (b) may not have the best sense of relative account quality to begin with. Having a great account scoring model certainly helps, but the best and more costly, option is having a strong, dedicated territory management function that vets, assigns, and refreshes a more reasonable set of accounts at any given time.

Regardless of which territory assignment approach you use with round-robin opportunity distribution, we recommend creating both a primary and secondary owner field: Account Owner and Engagement Owner, respectively. For AE prospected accounts, the AE should be assigned to both fields. For SDRs prospected accounts, the SDR should be the engagement owner and the account owner should be left blank. Once an SDR sources an opportunity, an account owner should be assigned by the round-robin algorithm. (Note: If account owner is a required field, then the SDR can be both the account owner and engagement owner until an opportunity is created and the account owner field is updated to an AE.)

Tip 8 : Have SDRs Source Their Own Contacts

As strongly as we advocate sourcing and assigning accounts for SDRs, there are also three major reasons we believe SDRs need to source their own contacts:

One, SDRs must comb through profile information as they personalize engagement.

Two, contacts move in and out of companies and titles/responsibilities are ever changing, so SDRs need correct information as they engage.

Three, we find centralized contact sourcing "engines" either over-source or become a bottleneck, both of which are costly.

(Note: Of course, SDRs need access to tools like LinkedIn Sales Navigator and ZoomInfo to source their own contacts.)

Tip 9: Seat SDRs with Each Other

While this final tip may come off as trivial, but we are often asked. whether or not SDRs should sit with each other or sit side-by-side with the AEs they support. The argument in favor of the integrated seating agreement goes like this:

For pods, you increase account coordination benefits.

For pods and pools, you increase the training and mentorship benefit for SDRs.

OK, you probably already know that it's our preference to cluster SDRs simply by this tip's title. It is not that the aforementioned benefits aren't valid, they are, but we feel the benefits of clustered seating are far stronger. In fact, seating SDRs with each other and their managers ensures:

(1.) rapid sharing of best practices among SDRs,

(2.) support for the sanctity of hunting blocks via social pressure and management pressure,

(3.) investment in team ethos,

(4.) managerial consistency and support.

CONCLUSION

CONCLUSION

We have now taken you deep into the art, backed by science, of leading exceptional sales development teams, however, not all art can be explained by science; at least not yet. One critical example of this is when two leaders take the same processes, people, and technologies and end up with entirely different results. This final chapter will offer our hypothesis as to why this happens.

Know Your People

A leader must develop the ability and the desire to know each of their people on a deep level. Like most leadership wisdom, this observation is not novel. We state it here to remind current and aspiring sales development leaders to devote themselves to this valuable practice. In our own cases we walk-the-walk ourselves by attempting to understand each SDR's personality using either the DISC or Social Styles[69] assessment which provide a person's primary and secondary working styles across four categories: dominance/driver, influence/expressive, support/amiable, and conscientiousness/analytical.

Know that there is no ideal leadership style and, for the record, Alea is a Driver and Jeremey is an Analytical. So instead of trying to attain a certain leadership style yourself, we recommend SDR leaders use their knowledge of each SDR's style to adapt and personalize their communication and coaching methods. Then to go even further and refine this directional understanding by having conversations with each SDR about what motivates each of them personally and professionally. Gain this knowledge allows leaders to customize optimal ways to provide feedback, inspire, and hold SDRs accountable.

Getting "meta," leaders must be open to feedback about giving feedback. Specifically, leaders must create a safe, bi-directional, communication culture. Imagine a leader with a dominance/driver personality style. While this type of leader might do their best to adapt to the styles of their SDRs when communicating one-on-one, the leader is human, too. Next imagine an SDR with the opposite style, support/amiable, who feels uncomfortable with a leader's direct, proactive approach. In this case any miscommunication is not because the leader is doing anything wrong; after all, they are consistent and professional with each team member. The point is that great leaders create environments in which SDRs with different styles are able to freely voice their feelings and be rewarded by the leader making a communication adjustment.

Recall that quotas should be set such that 70% of SDRs meet or exceed goal. We know that average SDR leaders keep all of their attention on SDRs who are below target, but great SDR leaders recognize they must continue to provide attention to those above target, since quota is a floor not a ceiling. If an SDR's talent allows them to hit 200%, the leader has a responsibility to invest in skill development and in motivation to help the associate attain the higher level of achievement.

This speaks to the broader concept of situational leadership[70]--coaching to the skill and the will of the individual on the given project at the given time. Every SDR is will have days and maybe even weeks when they are not performing up to par. In this case the SDR manager has a responsibility to exercise radical candor[71] by caring deeply enough to challenge directly. Stated another way, rekindling the spark that helps a struggling

SDR get back on track requires a person-specific balance of motivation (love) and accountability (tension).

Fine tuning your own interaction style to each SDR is not easy. It helps us to maintain a one-on-one document to capture notes, actions, and so on. Noting person's DISC/social style, as well as any key personal or professional goals that motivate them, lives at the top of this document. Then at the start of every one-on-one, a quick glance at the top of the page sets right communication mode. For tougher discussions outside of one-on-ones, such as those concerning performance gaps, we strive to pre-call plan, as we would before a client meeting, to map out the structure of and approach to the conversation.

Practice Accountability

Successful sales development leaders are comfortable holding their SDRs accountable. It is common for new managers to worry that accountability is tantamount to micromanagement, but in fact micromanagement gets its negative reputation from managers who do not set proper expectations or who intervene unnecessarily with skilled, motivated people. Managers who set achievable activity, effectiveness, and results targets not only have a right, but also have an obligation to hold the individuals on their teams accountable. They have an obligation to inspect what they expect.

As we have stressed throughout this book, the social contract between an SDR and manager is a two-way street in every respect and even a leader falls off their game from time to time. When this happens an SDR must feel just as safe in nudging their manager. A great manager responds by admitting they let the team down and then committing in word and in deed to getting back on the right path.

New managers often feel they must be perfect and have all the answers, however, they soon learn that no one is inspired by perfection-- or by cluelessness. Sales development leaders need to know the "why," the "what," and most of the "how." The "why" equates to the impact the sales development team has on the organization with career advancement for SDRs is being a major component. The "what" includes the activity, effectiveness, and results targets for the team. The "how" is where leaders need not be flawless. Yes, sales development leaders must know the levers that lead to success for the team and for every SDR. Take the example of A/B testing email messaging. The leader should know how to execute effective A/B tests, but need not be the sole fountain of wisdom of every messaging variation to test. It behooves any leader to cede a degree of creative control to SDRs as it encourages better ideas and keeps people engaged.

In our experience, leading sales development requires ongoing experimentation in every facet of strategy, including people, process, technology, and execution, including but not limited to cadence design, messaging, etc. The concept of needing to experiment is a "how." Managers who constantly initiate new tests keep their teams in a perpetual state of change. Whether this is ultimately effective or disruptive comes down to setting expectations.

That is why when new SDRs join our teams we tell them we abide by the old cliché' in that our only constant is change. We also invite everyone to bring new concepts to test. Our commitment to SDRs is that when we conduct an experiment, we promise to explain why we are doing it and what we will measure. Furthermore, we operate under the "obligation to dissent" principle. By this we mean that before we execute, SDRs are expected to voice their objections. Our response is to either adjust our approach or explain why we are unconcerned by a given objection. Once we start an initiative, however, the general dissent period ends, and we expect everyone to participate fully.

Inspire Followership Internally and Externally

Sales development leaders need to invest as much energy into authentic inspiration as they do into accountability. Above and beyond stoking the fires of individual intrinsic motivation, managers can inspire their teams by ensuring a clear line-of-sight between prospecting and business impact.

We let our SDRs know that we talk about their performance every week with our CROs and CEOs. SDRs benefit from frequent reminders of how important their work is to the success of the organization.

Most of what we have discussed in this book has been inward facing. In addition, outstanding sales development leaders must invest externally in their professional brand.

Two ways to attract and retain the best talent:
One. Sales development leaders must invest in the external reputation of their team. For example, one of our organizations has a monthly Pinnacle of Prospecting award for the top SDR. This award includes an obnoxiously large trophy the winner gets to display on their desk for the entire office to see. A picture of the winner is also posted on LinkedIn. We also make it a point to keep the winner informed of the magnitude of all of this exposure by sharing facts like, "Hey, 5,000 people looked at your Pinnacle of Prospecting post since yesterday. That's 5,000 people who know how excellent you are."

The benefits of promoting your best SDRs on social media far outweigh the risks. The first month we published the Pinnacle of Prospecting award on LinkedIn, the individual that won let us know that he really appreciated the post, but I didn't think it got the result that we expected. When we asked what he meant,

He said, "Well, because I've had a lot of recruiters reach out to me since you posted that."

We responded, "Well, of course! But in our opinion the world should know how excellent you are because you are very talented and you work hard to earn this acknowledgment. We're fine that recruiters at other organizations know about you. If we're doing our job by giving you a career path that motivates you, then you'll stay on our team to learn and grow into a highly successful AE." Do right by your people and they will stick with you. Do wrong by them and no amount of shielding them from recruiters will prevent them from leaving.

Team outings are another way to motivate and inspire your people. SDRs work hard and deserve to relax as a group. Celebrations also help SDRs bond with and get to know each other. But outings are not automatic; they are rewards granted when the entire team exceeds goals. Pro Tip: Since outings mean downtime, adjust goals so that celebrations are not the root cause of performance gaps.

Two. SDR leaders must invest in their own external reputations. Posting achievements of your SDRs on social media signals the fact that you care about and invest in your people. Beyond pictures, SDR leaders establish themselves as thought-leaders when they share best practices they learned from experimentation. Remember, quality trumps quantity. Do not be afraid to post every day if you have something important to say about sales development; otherwise, wait until you do. Offering value to the broader world via social media should lead to opportunities to speak at local events and perhaps at larger conferences.

And Lastly, Keep Your Team First

As a sales development leader, it is easy to get distracted by a whole host of priorities, many of which involve sitting in endless meetings with peers and superiors from across the organization. To combat this, you must create and respect weekly time-blocks to make sure and adhere to your commitments to hold people accountable, to inspire them, and to develop them. It is easy to view daily operating systems as important but not urgent. But, fight complacency. The care and feeding of your people is always your most important and urgent priority.

As we were writing this chapter, a colleague told us about an evening team outing he had long planned that illustrates our point perfectly. On the day of the event, as luck would have it, the CEO called him with an emergency. His initial instinct was to ask his team to enjoy their evening without him, but instead, realizing the importance of the evening, he called the CEO to negotiate delaying the requested action. By pointing out the delay would not incrementally impact clients, the CEO agreed.

In summarizing our ethos and the core message of our book, we want you to know that there is no bigger differentiator to your success as a sales development leader than the quality of the people that you attract, select, develop, hold accountable, inspire, and retain. Lead with science and systems and lead with art and love.

ACKNOWLEDGMENTS

To Michael for the love, the journey, and the empowerment.

To my family for the love and joy.

To all the exceptionally talented sales development reps that I've had the privilege of working with for the trust, passion, and inspiration.

To Jeremey for the friendship.

- AH

*   *   *   *   *

I'm upfront about the fact that live with an imposter complex when it comes to leading sales development because I've had a very non-traditional path into my treasured role. Specifically, my direct sales experience amounts to selling mangos as a child by the side of the road in Miami, Florida. Because of that, I'm enormously grateful to the scores of people who have taught me the art and science this profession. This includes too many colleagues, authors, and industry peers, to list.

Alea and I started in Sales Development at the same time and, not unexpectedly, she has far surpassed my knowledge and ability. One of the great joys in collaborating with her was the chance to learn new, high-impact approaches. As my team at SalesLoft knows, we put Alea's best practices in place as fast as the words flowed onto the pages of this book. Our performance accelerated with each initiative.

I'm also incredibly grateful to our pair of editors. My wife Irene read every word even though this brand of non-fiction is far from her cup of tea. PJ Dempsey, my faithful editor through six books, provided the final polish. Irene and PJ deserve credit for all proper grammar and great turns of phrase; I deserve all blame for any typos.

Finally, I'd like to thank my colleagues at SalesLoft. Our cofounders, Kyle and Rob, my boss Sean Murray and our executive team, and my 450+ coworkers prove daily that great culture and amazing business growth go hand-in-hand. #SalesLove

JD

ABOUT THE AUTHORS

Alea Homison is Vice President of Sales Enablement and Sales Development at AlphaSense where she is responsible for the development, acceleration, and optimization of talent across the sales and service organization. Alea specializes in building sales enablement programs for organizations focused on growth and scalability. She has developed and managed a variety of high performing teams throughout her career which spans sales, sales strategy, client service, corporate strategy, and investment banking. Alea holds an M.B.A. from Columbia Business School and a B.S. in Risk Management and Business from Gannon University.

Jeremey Donovan is SVP of Sales Strategy and Operations at SalesLoft, the world's leading sales engagement platform. Over the past 20+ years, he has had an eclectic career spanning semiconductor engineering to product development/management to sales & marketing leadership at Xilinx, Gartner, AMA, GLG, and CB Insights. Jeremey is the author of five books including the international public speaking bestseller "How to Deliver a TED Talk" as well as "Predictable Prospecting." He holds a BS and an MS in Electrical Engineering from Cornell University and an MBA from the University of Chicago Booth School of Business.

ENDNOTES

1   Schmidt, Frank L., and John E. Hunter. "The validity and utility of selection methods in personnel psychology: Practical and theoretical implications of 85 years of research findings." Psychological bulletin 124.2 (1998): 262.

2   Mussel, Patrick. "Introducing the construct curiosity for predicting job performance." Journal of Organizational Behavior 34.4 (2013): 453-472.

3   Duckworth, Angela L., et al. "Grit: perseverance and passion for long-term goals." Journal of personality and social psychology 92.6 (2007): 1087.

4   www.authentichappiness.org had 500,000 registered users when the study was conducted between April 2006 and September 2006.

5   Boushey, Heather, and Glynn, Sarah Jane. "There Are Significant Business Costs to Replacing Employees." November 16, 2012. https://www.americanprogress.org/wp-content/uploads/2012/11/CostofTurnover.pdf

6   We attribute this data to ETS even though the data is not directly available through ETS. https://www.statisticbrain.com/iq-estimates-by-intended-college-major/

7   https://www.nytimes.com/2013/06/20/business/in-head-hunting-big-data-may-not-be-such-a-big-deal.html?partner=socialflow&smid=tw-nytimesbusiness

8   Schmidt, Frank L., and John E. Hunter. "The validity and utility of selection methods in personnel psychology: Practical and theoretical implications of 85 years of research findings." Psychological bulletin 124.2 (1998): 262.

9   Schmidt, Frank L., and John E. Hunter. "The validity and utility of selection methods in personnel psychology: Practical and theoretical implications of 85 years of research findings." Psychological bulletin 124.2 (1998): 262.

10   Murphy, Nora A. "Appearing smart: The impression management of intelligence, person perception accuracy, and behavior in social interaction." Personality and Social Psychology Bulletin 33.3 (2007): 325-339.

11   https://www.nytimes.com/2013/06/20/business/in-head-hunting-big-data-may-not-be-such-a-big-deal.html?pagewanted=all

12   How Google Thinks About Hiring. Laszlo Bock being interviewed by KPCB General Partner Best Seidenberg. 2015. Time: 3:17-3:31.

13   Honer, Jeremiah, Chris W. Wright, and Chris J. Sablynski. "Puzzle interviews: What are they and what do they measure?." Applied HRM Research 11.2 (2007): 79.

14   Wonderlic Personnel Test & Scholastic Level Exam User's Manual. (2002). Libertyville, IL: Wonderlic.

15   https://www.criteriacorp.com/solution/ccat.php

16   https://www.joinkoru.com/

17   Bendick, Marc, and Ana P. Nunes. "Developing the research basis for controlling bias in hiring." Journal of Social Issues 68.2 (2012): 238-262.

18   Marlowe, Cynthia M., Sandra L. Schneider, and Carnot E. Nelson. "Gender and attractiveness biases in hiring decisions: Are more experienced managers less biased?." Journal of applied psychology 81.1 (1996): 11.

19   Pingitore, Regina, et al. "Bias against overweight job applicants in a simulated employment interview." Journal of applied psychology 79.6 (1994): 909.

20   Schmidt, Frank L., and John E. Hunter. "The validity and utility of selection methods in personnel psychology: Practical and theoretical

implications of 85 years of research findings." Psychological bulletin 124.2 (1998): 262.

21   https://rework.withgoogle.com/blog/google-rule-of-four/

22   https://rework.withgoogle.com/blog/the-evolution-of-project-oxygen/

23   https://careers.google.com/how-we-hire/interview/

24   https://medium.com/google-design/what-i-learned-from-interviewing-and-receiving-offers-from-google-two-times-e1d1a7b715bc

25   https://rework.withgoogle.com/guides/hiring-use-structured-interviewing/steps/use-a-grading-rubric/

26   Smart, Bradford D., and Greg Alexander. Topgrading for Sales: World-Class Methods to Interview, Hire, and Coach Top Sales Representatives. Portfolio, 2008.

27   Lorence, Michael S. "The Impact of Systematically Hiring Top Talent: A Study of Topgrading as a Rigorous Employee Selection Bundle." (2014).

28   https://www.glassdoor.com/Reviews/SalesLoft-Reviews-E759703.htm

29   Cerasoli, Christopher P., Jessica M. Nicklin, and Michael T. Ford. "Intrinsic motivation and extrinsic incentives jointly predict performance: A 40-year meta-analysis." Psychological Bulletin 140.4 (2014): 980.

30   Source: GlassDoor, October 21, 2018

31   Gottlieb, Dan. TOPO 2019 Sales Development Benchmark Report. Page 17.

32   Gottlieb, Dan. TOPO 2019 Sales Development Benchmark Report. Page 34.

33   Gottlieb, Dan. TOPO 2019 Sales Development Benchmark Report. Page 24.

34   To make this calculation possible, we used 50% for the below 50% category, 120% for the 100% or above category, and the mid-points of the given ranges for the other categories.

35   Statisticians will object the distribution is left-skewed and cut off at zero. While true, it is easier to model and explain using a normal distribution and the result works out almost the same with a more complex probability distribution function.

36   Gottlieb, Dan. TOPO 2019 Sales Development Benchmark Report. Page 13.

37   Source: GlassDoor, July 14, 2019

38   We define Sales Accepted Leads as meetings set, held, and not immediately disqualified by AEs.

39   Sales Development 2018: Metrics and Compensation Research Report, The Bridge Group Inc.

40   The benchmark report has 11 SALs per month but we've more commonly seen 10 for outbound SDRs. Similarly, the report has $2.7M of pipeline generated per month but we rounded to $3M for convenience.

41   For your business, consider backing into the pipeline target as follows. Imagine you want your SDRs to be responsible for sourcing $600K of closed-won business. Further assuming a 20% close rate from early-stage opportunities, one needs SDRs to create $600k/0.2 = $2.7M of pipeline per year, or $250K/month.

42   Equal business stature is a concept from Sandler training used to describe the ideal relationship between AEs and prospect. We leverage this language to describe the ideal relationship between SDRs and AEs.

43   Slavin, Robert E. "When does cooperative learning increase student achievement?" Psychological bulletin 94.3 (1983): 429.

44   Dave Fischer

45   (D)ominance, (I)nfluence, (S)teadiness, (C)onscientiousness

46   https://www.paceproductivity.com/single-post/2017/02/09/How-Sales-Reps-Spend-Their-Time. This rate is for salespeople in general. Though we were unable to obtain SDR specific benchmarks, we have observed rates of around 40%.

47   TOPO 2016 Sales Development Benchmark Report

48   More precisely, one wants to compare positive reply rates. However, natural language processing algorithms are not yet all that great at detecting positive email replies. All is not lost because one can reasonably assume that the portion of negative replies is probably about the same for the A and the B.

49   Here is the online calculator we use: https://www.socscistatistics.com/tests/ztest/default2.aspx

50   We have benchmarked our own teams and found between 50% and 70% but we decided to use a lower number to be conservative. This compares favorably to benchmarks of AE/AM selling time of around 35%.

51   "It's Not Business… It's Personal" - Corporate Visions 2019. Authors: Tim Riesterer, Leslie Talbot, and Steve Jones.

52   Click-through rate = clicks divided by opens

53   Meeting rate = meetings divided by opens

54   Source: SalesLoft call analysis, 2019

55   Downing, J. R. "Linking Communication Competence with Call Center Agents' Sales Effectiveness." Journal of Business Communication, vol. 48, no. 4, pp. 409–425.

56   While we could not locate academic research to justify this guidance, having SDRs state their full names is grounded in convention wisdom and feels helpful or harmless to us.

57   Tip #4 in https://www.gong.io/blog/cold-calling-tips/

58   Tip #3 in https://www.gong.io/blog/cold-calling-tips/

59   A Sandler Training framework.

60   State of Conversation Intelligence 2020: Top Habits of High Growth Sales Teams. Chorus.

61   State of Conversation Intelligence 2020: Top Habits of High Growth Sales Teams. Chorus.

62   State of Conversation Intelligence 2020: Top Habits of High Growth Sales Teams. Chorus. Page 17.

63   State of Conversation Intelligence 2020: Top Habits of High Growth Sales Teams. Chorus. Page 16.

64   TOPO 2019 Sales Development Benchmark Report page 13 show an SDR-sourced opportunity close rate of 21%. We nudged down to a slightly more conservative 20% to keep our calculations cleaner.

65   Sales Development 2018 Metrics and Compensation Report. The Bridge Group.Page 44. The benchmark is 21 meetings passed per month per SDR but we rounded down to the more conservative 20.

66   Fringe costs include benefits and payroll taxes.

67   Sales Development 2018 Metrics and Compensation Report. The Bridge Group.Page 59.Average organizations spend $371 per month per SDR ($4,452 per year) and high-growth organizations spend 10% more ($4,897). We rounded up a bit to yield a more conservative ROI calculation.

68   Sales Development 2018 Metrics & Compensation Research Report, The Bridge Group, Inc.

69   Merrill, D. W. and Reid, R. H. (1999). Personal styles and effective performance. New York: CRC Press.

70   Blanchard, Kenneth H. The One Minute Manager. [New York] :Morrow, an imprint of HarperCollinsPublisher, 2003.

71   Scott, Kim Malone. Radical Candor: How to Be a Kickass Boss Without Losing Your Humanity. First edition. New York: St. Martin's Press, 2017.